The Pleasure of Whole-Grain Breads

The Pleasure
of Whole-Grain Breads

by Beth Hensperger

Photographs by Daniel Clark

CHRONICLE BOOKS
SAN FRANCISCO

Library of Congress Cataloging-in-Publication Data available.

ISBN 0-8118-1455-6

Printed in Hong Kong.

Food & Prop styling by Ethel Brennan.
Designed by Shawn Hazen.
Photographer's acknowledgements: I wish to give thanks to my wife, Laura, for inspiration and constant support. To my kids, Ellis and Paris, and our special friend Beverly. And last, to Ethel— great work!

Photograph facing title page: Barley Buttermilk Bread.

Distributed in Canada by Raincoast Books
8680 Cambie Street
Vancouver, British Columbia V6P 6M9

10 9 8 7 6 5 4 3 2 1

Chronicle Books
85 Second Street
San Francisco, California 94105   www.chroniclebooks.com

Acknowledgements

Many people have helped me during the writing of this cookbook, and I wish to express my appreciation.

Thanks to my super-agent Martha Casselman, for her continuing interest, appropriate suggestions, and generous friendship. Her fine analytical and creative hand is evident throughout this book.

Thanks to my editors and advisors, Sarah Putman, Stephanie Rosenbaum, and Bill LeBlond, for their guidance, helpful recommendations, and countless hours of hard work. Thank you to Judith Dunham for her editing skills.

Special thanks for the expertise given to me by Lynn Alley of Lost Arts Trading Company; Emigdio Ballon, Inca and High Elevation Crop Specialist and Research Associate, Seeds of Change; Robert Barker and the Fitzhugh Ludlow Memorial Library archives; "Mr. Teff," Wayne Carlson; Jean Clem of Western Trails Food Products; Susan Derecskey for her review of early material; Lynda Glenn of Arrowhead Mills; Al Guisto of Guisto's Flour; Bonnie Fernandez of the California Wheat Commission; Dr. Lee Jackson, U.C. Davis Grain Specialist; Grace Kirschenbaum and the World of Cookbooks; food writer Rachel Albert Matisse; Dr. Dwain Meyer, Department of Plant Science, Northern Crops Institute at North Dakota State University; Virginia New of White Mountain Farms; Alice Pearson of Red Star Yeast & Products; Toni Ramsaur of Gibbs Wild Rice; Rodale Institute Research Center; Brinna Sands of King Arthur Flour; Lorenz Schaller and the KUSA Seed Society; Larry Walters of Nu-World Amaranth, Inc.; and the Zojirushi America Corporation.

Profound thanks to my team of kitchen witches for testing and taking time to give valuable feedback: Lynn Alley, Sallie Ford Doeg, Sarah Dreher, Mary Anne McCready, Marie Meseroll, Berit Meyer, Lou Seibert Pappas, Tracey M. Sutton, and Bobbe Torgerson.

Contents

Grains and Recipes

The Seed As Perfect Food

When I started baking bread, I never imagined becoming so fascinated with the world of grains. I first used the grains that nourished me since childhood—the familiar wheat, rice, and corn—then turned to eating and baking with other forms of these familiar grains, which quickly became favorites. Friends served homey breads I was quick to adopt into my repertoire: Scandinavian rye from Minnesota, white corn bread from South Carolina, thick johnnycake pancakes from Rhode Island, sourdough bread from well-used Alaskan starter, soda bread from Ireland, tandoor-baked *naan* from India, and delectable *sopaipillas* from Mexico. From there it was only a short step to using less common grains such as blue corn, quinoa, amaranth, kamut, spelt, and teff.

The word *cereal* refers to all food-grain-bearing grass. It is derived from the summer celebration of Cerealia, in honor of Ceres, Roman goddess of the crops and Great Mother of the Harvest. The word *ceres* was often used by the early Romans to mean a loaf of baked bread. Over the centuries, cereal has endured as the common word for grains in the Gramineae family, which includes wheat, barley, rye, rice, millet, buckwheat, and corn. Delicious flours are also made from edible tubers (potatoes, Jerusalem artichokes, cassava), nuts and pods (chestnuts, acorns, carob, almonds, mesquite), legumes (peas, lentils, soybeans, chickpeas,

lima beans, fava beans), and rice. Some of these flours are familiar, while others, though unfamiliar, are an integral part of cuisines of other cultures. Many of these old-fashioned flours are experiencing a renaissance in breads made for gluten-free diets.

Bread baking has been described as an art form because it is a process that combines all of the senses with the goal of producing food for physical nourishment. It is no wonder that the rise of grain agriculture parallels the development of civilization. The great cultures of antiquity grew up around areas where cereal grains were grown, referred to as hearths of domestication, giving rise to many scholarly debates of when and why humans turned from being hunters and gatherers to settled agriculturalists. All the practical implications aside, there can be no generalizations on the complex factors that brought about the domestication of grain crops. Speaking simply, however, life as we know it would certainly be impossible without cereal grains.

Many years ago I was advised by my physician that instead of eating wheat products on a daily basis, I should alternate wheat with other grains every other day to prevent a grain allergy. At the time, the concept seemed novel; I was familiar only with corn tortillas and Jewish rye bread as alternatives. As I discovered, embarking on any dietary change takes some planning and personal discipline. But with an increased serious interest in nutrition, more individuals are taking charge of contributing to their own good health. Grains now found in greater variety at most supermarkets, not only natural-food stores, are part of a sound nutritional plan.

When you use whole-grain flours rather than refined flours, you take advantage of all parts of the grain: the fiber-rich bran, the vitamin-rich germ, and the protein-rich starch. Each grain is a tiny dry fruit that contains a single seed capable of reproducing itself. An inedible, hard outer shell called the hull protects the seed and must be removed to make the seed available for cooking or grinding. The seed is surrounded by a layer of starchy carbohydrates designed to feed a developing embryo. The embryo, or germ, contains a concentration of micronutrients, fat, and proteins. It is rich in vitamins E, A, and B-complex, protein, calcium, and iron. The outer coating, the bran, provides fiber and is composed of cellulose, a complex sugar. Grains are high in valuable water-soluble fiber, a major source of complex carbohydrates and a gold mine of minerals. In varying amounts, they contain all ten essential amino acids. The New World's "lost" sacred grains, amaranth and quinoa, are known for their high percentage of lysine, an essential amino acid lacking in all other grains.

During the digestion process, grains provide an even flow of energy and stamina and absorb water, creating that full feeling. They are also free of cholesterol and low in fat. Most people are well acquainted with the virtues of whole grains through the highly advertised need for more dietary fiber. Known as roughage, fiber in the form of pectin gums and brans is the indigestible part of a plant food, the amount and type of fiber varying from plant to plant.

As the recipes in this book show, whole-wheat bread can be made from kamut, spelt, or semolina. The addition of other whole grains and specialty flours to wheat flour creates loaves with an irresistible variety of flavors, aromas, and textures: wild rice and rye, corn-meal millet, sprouted wheat berry, oatmeal whole wheat, teff honey egg. Multigrain breads are wildly popular, and in this book, you will find recipes for both yeast loaves and quick breads featuring all sorts of whole grains. You don't need to know how to make yeast breads to make loaves with delicious grain combinations. Quick loaves, pancakes, muffins, and scones can be made with whole grains. If you are looking for instant nutrition, whole grains can give it to you. And they taste good, too.

Bread-Making Basics

Bread-Making Basics

The following information is invaluable for choosing ingredients, mixing, shaping, and baking doughs and batters, and storing breads. Baking with whole grains is different from using all-white flour: whole-grain flours absorb more liquid, require a bit more leavening power, take more muscle to knead, and take longer to rise.

Ingredients

If you are buying whole grains in bulk, avoid grains that seem too dried out or soggy, or contain larvae—problems that can occur when grains are not stored properly directly after harvest. Unground whole grains have a long shelf life—about one year—when stored in moisture-proof airtight containers or sealable thick plastic bags, out of direct light and at a cool room temperature. Unbleached flour keeps up to one year in a tightly closed container at room temperature. Whole-grain flours should be stored in tightly closed containers in the refrigerator for up to three months or in the freezer for up to nine months. If flours and meals are stone-ground and contain the germ and bran, they are highly perishable. Corn, oat, rice, barley, and wheat brans should be stored in the refrigerator for six to eight months; raw and toasted wheat germ is best refrigerated and used within three to four months.

If a flour or grain is rancid, it will have a definite sour smell. Remember to label and date stored flours; it is amazing how similar they look.

Yeast needs to be dissolved and activated in warm liquids. Liquids should be 90° to 120°F, or feel comfortably warm on the back of your hand or inside of your wrist. Water that is too hot will kill the yeast; water that is too cold will delay the action. It is advisable to invest in a yeast thermometer until you can recognize the exact warmth by feel.

All types of yeast are interchangeable. An envelope of active dry yeast (a scant tablespoon) is equal to a .66-ounce cake of compressed yeast. One .66-ounce cake of compressed yeast is equal to 2 teaspoons instant dry yeast. One .25-ounce package of active dry yeast (a scant tablespoon) is equal to 2 teaspoons of instant dry yeast.

To substitute honey and other liquid-based sweeteners like molasses for granulated sugar, use three-quarters cup honey for each cup of sugar and reduce the total liquid used in the recipe by a quarter cup. For recipes in which no liquid is required, compensate by adding an extra quarter-cup flour. Avoid sugar substitutes in baking; they can't withstand the heat and tend to have a bitter, chemical aftertaste. Naturally sweet flours such as oat, barley, chestnut, and white whole wheat reduce the need for sugar.

Many expert whole-grain bakers swear by the addition of vital wheat gluten, a premium dough conditioner, to make an elastic dough that rises high. Add one and a half teaspoons vital wheat gluten for each cup of whole-wheat flour; add two to three teaspoons vital wheat gluten for each cup of glutenless flours such as barley, oats, rye, or soy.

The quantity of flour used in a recipe can vary according to weather conditions. In hot, humid climates, dough might require a bit more flour. Dough will absorb slightly different amounts of unbleached flour depending on the weather conditions where the wheat was grown and the type of specialty flour used.

Kneading and Rising

When kneading dough, beginning bakers often add too much flour. Adding too much flour results in a dough that is slack, cold, and tough. Too little flour and the dough has sticky spots.

Knead dough only until it retains a moist, tacky quality, yet feels smooth when you run your hand over the surface. It should hold its shape and be springy to the touch. Leave whole-wheat dough sticky; it will firm up as it rises. If it is still too moist, add a few tablespoons of flour after the rise. Doughs with flaked grains, such as rolled oats or barley, wheat, or quinoa flakes, have a nubby feel. The addition of cornmeal, barley grits, and small raw grains, such as millet, quinoa, and teff, make a dough that is gritty or pebbly to the touch. Using cooked grains makes a slightly lumpy dough.

The longer that dough slowly rises at room temperature, the more developed the flavor will be and lighter the texture. Never desert a very slow dough; whole-grain doughs take from one hour to four hours to rise. Dough generally rises to no more than double in bulk; occasional exceptions are noted in specific recipes. Never overrise these doughs.

Many expert bakers refrigerate dough overnight as a standard procedure, as dough that rises slowly develops the best flavor and texture. Yeast dough may be refrigerated at any time during the rising process: after kneading, after the first rise, or even after being shaped. Place the dough ball in a well-greased deep container and cover with two layers of plastic wrap. Water-based doughs keep up to four days and milk-based doughs up to two to three days in the refrigerator with frequent punching down during the first six hours. Let the chilled dough stand at room temperature for thirty minutes before proceeding.

Baking

Oven temperature is crucial when baking whole-grain loaves. An oven that is too hot will result in an overdone crust and underdone interior; too cool, a dense,

Using a Bread Machine

If you plan to make breads rich with whole grains and sticky starters, you must own a machine that has specific settings for them. The machines that outperform the rest at this writing are the Zojirushi (the "Zo"); Home Bakery BCC-15 and BBC-V20; Breadman TR800; Welbilt ABM7500; and Toastmaster Breadmaker's Hearth Breadmaker and Cook's Oven 1193. All have a strong kneading action and are able to work the stiffest doughs; many have a Dough Only setting for overnight starters.

- Read the recipe carefully and never exceed the capacity of your machine for best results. Follow exactly the manufacturer's instructions and recipe guidelines for your model. Check the recipe format in this book against the instructions for your machine; some models take a dash more yeast or a tablespoon or two more liquid.

- All bread machine models require the use of active dry yeast.

- Layer the ingredients according to the manufacturer's instructions. In the delayed cycle, layer the yeast and dry milk in the bottom of the baking cylinder. It is important that they do not touch the liquid.

- Hold back ¼ cup flour when loading the canister. Check the dough consistency after the first 10 minutes; if the dough is too moist, add the additional flour.

- Small machines make a 1-pound loaf, yielding about 8 slices (perfect for two people). They have the capacity for ¾ to 1 cup liquid and 2 to 3 cups flour, which means that most traditional yeast bread recipes calling for 5 to 6 cups flour need to be divided in half. This total amount of flour includes any other dry ingredients (except dry milk powder) such as bran, whole-wheat flour, oatmeal, and other specialty flours. Larger machines use 1½ cups liquid to 4 cups of flour to make close to a 1½-pound loaf, yielding about 12 slices. To make a 2-pound loaf in the largest machines, double the quantities used for a 1-pound loaf.

- The best loaves are made with a high proportion of high-gluten bread flour; this helps to ensure a loaf that is not too dense. Add 1½ teaspoons to 1 tablespoon of vital wheat gluten per 1 cup flour. Loaves with whole-grain flours or meals will always be more compact in texture than loaves made entirely of white flour.

- Machine-made bread is best eaten the same day it is made, as the loaves dry out quickly.

Milling Flour

If you become a serious baker of whole-grain bread, the allure of milling grains will eventually call to you. Owning and operating a home grain mill are an investment in time and money, but have notable advantages.

When you mill your own grains, a minimal time lapses between milling the grain and mixing the dough. Bakers who engage in this old-fashioned task swear by the flavor and texture of their breads. I had always heard that aging improves flour performance, but whole-grain flours actually begin to deteriorate as soon as they are ground. So in this case, fresh is best. Another advantage is that you can buy whole grains and grind them in different textures, depending on your needs.

There is a practical model of grain mill for every bread baker's taste, aesthetics, and pocketbook. My first mill was the very heavy, rustic cast-stone Samap hand mill. Operating it was tremendously laborious, but was a very artistic way to grind coarse grains. The counter-clamped steel Corona hand mill for making *masa* and cracked grains graced all early back-to-the-earth kitchens; grains had to be ground many times to get even a coarse texture. Today a grain enthusiast who wants commercial mill quality should try one of the efficient plastic-bodied electric mills, like the Magic Mill or the Whisper Mill, which grind hard wheat berries, soybeans, and corn kernels perfectly in one grinding. KitchenAid offers a grain mill attachment with steel blades for their heavy-duty electric mixers, and Braun has a small electric mill.

Grind settings on mills for home use range from very coarse to very fine. Large grains (wheat, corn, rye) yield one cup flour per one cup whole grain. Small grains (amaranth, teff, rice, millet) yield one cup flour per three-quarters cup whole grain.

dry loaf. Resist the temptation to open the oven door during the first fifteen minutes, to prevent the bread from collapsing.

Bread is not finished baking until it has cooled, allowing the crumb to set and the excess moisture to evaporate (hot bread weighs more than a cooled loaf). This is especially important for whole-grain breads. Let loaves rest for at least thirty minutes. Breads are best served warm, at room temperature, or reheated.

Storing Bread

Whole-grain loaves have a good shelf life and do not go stale quickly. They generally stay moist for about three days. Store enclosed in plastic wrap, at room temperature. Sweet breads and breads containing cheese fillings or dairy products should be refrigerated.

To freeze bread, wrap first in plastic wrap, then in a layer of aluminum foil (to prevent freezer burn). Or, wrap in a double layer of lock-top plastic freezer bags. It must be completely cool, or the center will freeze solid and later defrost into a soggy mass. Label and date the package. Freeze two to three months.

To thaw frozen bread, defrost in the wrapping at room temperature for at least three hours, shaking out any accumulated ice crystals. Unwrap and reheat at the temperature at which the bread was baked for about eight to ten minutes. Bread may be refreshed or thawed in a 325°F oven for twenty to forty minutes, or until heated through. If the bread is unwrapped, the crust will crisp. Rolls are best reheated wrapped since they tend to dry out more quickly than loaves.

Grains and Recipes

Amaranth

Along with buckwheat and quinoa, amaranth is one of the very few non-grasses to yield edible grain seeds. The plant has gigantic seed heads (up to half a million per plant), and its spinachlike leaves and stems vary in color from purple and red to gold and white. The genus name, *Amaranthus,* means "everlasting or unfading," probably a reference to the jewellike colors of the seed heads when dried. Amaranth belongs to a group of super-performers categorized by botanists as C4 and including the world's fastest-growing crops, which also have the advantage of quickly adapting to environmental changes.

The genus is so large that there are plants grown specifically for dyes, colorful ornamentals (cockscomb and love-lies-bleeding), and vegetables as well as grains. Wild species are distributed all over the world. Although amaranth is considered a New World grain, it is recorded as *ramdana,* "seed sent by God," in old Sanskrit records, and hundreds of strains dot the Himalayas, where it is a favorite crop of today's hill farmers. In China, the grain was known as "the thousand-ear cereal," and in the Andes as "Incan wheat." For the ancient Mayans, it was a medicinal and religious staple.

Amaranth was gathered as a staple food by the early cave dwellers of the Americas and by the nomadic native tribes of the Southwest just a hundred years ago.

It is among the thirty thousand plant fragments found at Meadowcroft Rockshelter on the Ohio River, the earliest occupied site in the United States, first settled over twelve thousand years ago.

Cultivated in conjunction with maize and bean crops, amaranth was used to make tortillalike flatbreads, and was fed to runner messengers and soldiers going into battle. A paste of the ground seeds, *zoale,* was fashioned into honey cakes in the shape of Aztec deities and consumed by worshipers. When Hernando Cortés conquered the Aztecs in 1519, he destroyed the massive fields of grain amaranth and forbid the cultivation and consumption of the sacred grain. Cortés took the seed back to Spain, and from there the grain spread to Africa and India.

Amaranth has experienced a contemporary resurgence of interest. In 1976, a food technologist named Larry Walters attended a seminar on amaranth hosted by John Rodale of the Rodale Research Institute in Pennsylvania. Walters planted his first crop, with seeds obtained from Rodale, in Earlsville, Iowa, in 1980. His company, Nu-World Amaranth, Inc., was born when an article in the February 1982 *Organic Gardening* magazine listed him as a purveyor. Today his company is the main source for growing, processing, distributing, marketing, and educating the public about the grain.

High in calcium and phosphorus, amaranth contains approximately sixteen percent protein, which is concentrated in the germ. It has two times more protein than cereals such as corn or barley. The only grain to contain vitamin C, it also boasts a high proportion of lysine, an essential amino acid rarely found in vegetable matter.

Amaranth seeds are minute golden-beige dots the size of a grain of sand, flecked with black and tan. They have a strong, sweet, wild grassy flavor likened to the taste of fresh corn silk. When toasted, the seeds mellow to a mild nutty flavor. When cooked, amaranth has a rather gelatinous, yet crunchy, grits-like texture and a transparent appearance. Adding the warm cooked grain to yeast and cornmeal batters helps baked goods retain moisture and lightness.

Amaranth flour is great in combination with high-protein wheat flour in yeast breads and can be used interchangeably with teff flour to add a distinctly peppery taste to baked goods. At most, use a one-to-four ratio of amaranth flour to wheat flour, or one cup amaranth flour to four cups wheat flour. The flour is also excellent in quick breads such as muffins, pancakes, and waffles. If you cannot find the flour, whole seeds can be ground in a flour mill, or amaranth seed, cooked whole like rice, can be added to bread doughs. While the seeds can be ground in a food processor or blender, a steel mill is the only efficient method I have found that successfully breaks the tough seed coat. Amaranth is never stone-ground, as mill stones cannot be set close enough to grind flour, and the result is gritty.

Types of Products

Whole amaranth seed is the whole unhulled grain. It is so tiny that it is never hulled. Amaranth flour is finely ground raw or toasted whole amaranth.

Along with quinoa and buckwheat, amaranth is another great nonwheat flour that has found a place in the baker's repertoire. This is a high-protein bread that tastes rich and homey. Delicious toasted, it is also excellent served with warm chèvre and a salad.

Amaranth Seed Bread

Makes two 9-by-5-inch loaves

 3½ to 4¼ cups bread flour

 1½ cups amaranth flour

 1½ cups whole-wheat flour

 2 tablespoons sesame seeds

 2 tablespoons poppyseeds

 1 tablespoon flax seeds

 1 tablespoon toasted whole amaranth seeds (see page 22)

 ½ cup dry buttermilk powder

 1 tablespoon (1 package) active dry yeast

 1 tablespoon salt

 2½ cups hot water (120°F)

 3 tablespoons unsalted butter, melted

 ⅓ cup dark molasses

1. In a large bowl using a whisk or in the bowl of a heavy-duty electric mixer fitted with the paddle attachment, combine 1 cup of the bread flour and the amaranth and whole-wheat flours, sesame, poppy, flax, and amaranth seeds, buttermilk powder, yeast, and salt. Add the hot water. Beat hard for about 2 minutes. Add the melted butter and molasses; beat 1 minute longer. Add the remaining bread flour, ½ cup at a time, beating on low speed until a soft, shaggy dough that just clears the sides of the bowl forms, switching to a wooden spoon when necessary if making by hand.

2. Turn the dough out onto a lightly floured work surface and knead until the dough is soft, sticky, and elastic and holds its shape, 1 to 3 minutes for a machine-mixed dough and 4 to 7 minutes for a hand-mixed dough, dusting with flour only 1 tablespoon at a time, just enough as needed to prevent sticking. Place in a lightly greased deep container, turn once to coat the top, and cover with plastic wrap. Let rise at room temperature until double in bulk, 1½ to 2 hours.

3. Grease the bottom and sides of two 9-by-5-inch loaf pans (I like to use terra-cotta pans). Turn the dough out onto a clean work surface and divide into 2 equal portions. Pat each portion into a rectangle and roll into a loaf shape. Place the loaves, seam side down, into the prepared pans. Cover loosely with plastic wrap and let rise until the dough is puffy and about 1 inch above the rims of the pans, about 45 minutes.

4. About 20 minutes before baking, preheat an oven to 350°F and position a rack in the center of the oven.

5. Using a sharp knife, make 3 diagonal slashes no more than ¼ inch deep down the top center of the loaf. Bake for 35 to 40 minutes, or until the tops are deep brown, the sides slightly contract from the pan, and the loaves sound hollow when tapped with your finger. Remove from the pans to cool on a rack.

Bread-Machine Amaranth Seed Bread

1½-pound loaf

1¼ cups water

2 tablespoons unsalted butter, melted

3 tablespoons molasses

1½ cups bread flour

¾ cup amaranth flour

¾ cup whole-wheat flour

⅓ cup dry buttermilk powder

1½ tablespoons vital wheat gluten

1 tablespoon plus 1 teaspoon sesame seeds

1 tablespoon plus 1 teaspoon poppyseeds

2 teaspoons flax seeds

2 teaspoons toasted whole amaranth seeds (see page 22)

1¼ teaspoons salt

2 teaspoons bread machine yeast

1-pound loaf

⅞ cup water

1½ tablespoons unsalted butter, melted

2 tablespoons molasses

1 cup bread flour

½ cup amaranth flour

½ cup whole-wheat flour

¼ cup dry buttermilk powder

1 tablespoon vital wheat gluten

1 tablespoon sesame seeds

1 tablespoon poppyseeds

1½ teaspoons flax seeds

1½ teaspoons toasted whole amaranth seeds (see page 22)

¾ teaspoon salt

1½ teaspoons bread machine yeast

1. Place all of the ingredients in the pan according to the manufacturer's instructions. Set crust on medium and program for the whole-wheat bread cycle; press Start. If using the basic bread cycle, after the first rise cycle, reset, allowing the dough to rise a second time.

2. After the baking cycle ends, remove the bread from the pan and place on a rack to cool to room temperature before slicing.

English muffins belong on a list of specialty breads from the British Isles that reads like a cast of rascals from Shakespeare's A Midsummer Night's Dream: crumpets, huffkins, pikelets, whiggs, splits, baps, rowies, singing hinnies, and rastons. Use commercial muffin rings 3 inches in diameter and 1¾ inch deep, or 7½-ounce pineapple or 6⅛-ounce tuna cans with the tops and bottoms removed. Split the muffins with a fork, so that the butter has lots of little pockets in which to puddle.

Oven-Baked Four-Grain English Muffins

Makes fourteen 3-inch muffins

1 cup warm water (105° to 115°F)

1¼ tablespoons (1¼ packages) active dry yeast

2 tablespoons packed light brown sugar

2 tablespoons raw whole millet

¼ cup oat bran

¼ cup rolled oats

⅓ cup whole-wheat flour

½ cup amaranth flour

3½ to 4 cups unbleached all-purpose flour

2 teaspoons salt

1 large egg

1¼ cups warm milk (105° to 115°F)

¼ cup canola oil

About ½ cup farina, for sprinkling

1. Pour the warm water into a small bowl. Sprinkle the yeast and a pinch of the sugar over the water. Stir to dissolve and let stand at room temperature until foamy, about 10 minutes.

2. In a large bowl using a whisk or in the bowl of a heavy-duty electric mixer fitted with the paddle attachment, stir together the remaining sugar, millet, bran, oats, whole-wheat and amaranth flours, 1 cup of the all-purpose flour, and salt. Make a well in the center and add the egg, milk, oil, and yeast mixture. Beat hard for about 2 minutes. Add the remaining all-purpose flour, ½ cup at a time, mixing on low speed until a soft dough that pulls from the sides of the bowl in long strands forms, switching to a wooden spoon when necessary if making by hand. The batter will be thick, soft, and sticky, which is important for creating a light-textured muffin; it will not be thick enough for kneading. Place in a lightly greased deep container, cover with a double layer of plastic wrap, and refrigerate for 8 hours, or as long as overnight.

3. Line a heavy-gauge baking sheet with parchment paper and sprinkle generously with farina. Grease 14 muffin rings 3 inches in diameter and 1½ inches deep and dip each ring in the farina. Arrange on the prepared baking sheet. Stir down the batter and turn out onto a clean plastic cutting board. Divide into 14 equal portions and place into the prepared rings. Sprinkle the tops with farina. Cover loosely with plastic wrap and let rise at room temperature until double in bulk, about 1 hour.

4. About 20 minutes before baking, preheat an oven to 400°F and position a rack on the lowest level of the oven.

5. Bake the muffins until puffy and brown and the tops feel dry and springy, 20 to 25 minutes. Place the baking sheet on a rack to cool for 10 minutes. Loosen the muffins from the rings and remove to the rack to cool. Cooled English muffins can be frozen for up to 2 months.

These "new-fashioned" whole-grain waffles are healthy and have a crunchy texture. Cornmeal, amaranth, and wheat are a particularly harmonious combination of grains. Toasting whole amaranth is important, as the seed coat is quite indigestible. When heated, the seeds pop like kernels of popcorn. Serve the waffles with sweet butter or equal amounts of whipped crème fraîche and vanilla yogurt folded together to make a fluffy, rich topping.

Three-Grain Vanilla Waffles

Makes 6 to 8 large waffles

1¼ cups unbleached all-purpose flour

¾ cup yellow cornmeal, preferably stone-ground and fine-grind

⅔ cup amaranth flour

2 tablespoons toasted whole amaranth seeds (see Note)

3 tablespoons packed light brown sugar

1 teaspoon baking powder

1 teaspoon baking soda

¼ teaspoon salt

2 large eggs

1 teaspoon pure vanilla extract

2¼ cups buttermilk

6 tablespoons unsalted butter, melted

Oil or melted butter, for greasing waffle iron

1. In a large bowl, combine the all-purpose flour, cornmeal, amaranth flour, toasted amaranth seeds, sugar, baking powder, baking soda, and salt. In another bowl, combine the eggs, vanilla, and buttermilk with a whisk until foamy. Pour into the dry ingredients and combine with a few strokes. Drizzle with the 6 tablespoons melted butter and fold in until the batter is just evenly moistened; do not overmix.

2. Preheat a waffle iron to medium-high heat or according to the manufacturer's instructions. Grease the hot waffle iron grids with oil or melted butter. For each waffle, pour about 1 cup batter onto the grid. Close the lid and bake until the waffle is crisp and well browned, 4 to 5 minutes. Remove from the iron with a fork. Serve immediately, or cool completely on racks, store in plastic bags, and freeze for up to 2 months.

To Toast Whole Amaranth Seeds:
Place a heavy saucepan over medium heat. Add the amaranth seeds, 1 tablespoon at a time, to the hot pan. Toast, stirring constantly with a wooden spoon, until the seeds pop like tiny kernels of popcorn. Remove from the pan. Continue toasting the seeds in batches to avoid overcrowding the pan. The seeds quadruple in volume when toasted; 1 tablespoon raw seeds yields ¼ cup toasted seeds.

Barley

One of the first domesticated grains, barley is, along with wheat, one of the foremost members of the Gramineae family. It grows to almost three feet in height and can be planted in the spring or fall. With its symmetrical rows of kernels and beautiful long beards, barley looks much like wheat. Types of barley are distinguished by their hulls, whether they are loose fitting or tightly attached. The hull-less varieties originated in prehistoric times in the mountains of China, and the hulled varieties, commonly grown in Europe, hail from the Middle East and North Africa.

The oldest text to mention a grain of any kind is the set of Babylonian clay tablets known as the Code of Hammurabi, which lists the agricultural taxes set on barley crops. The Babylonians used barley as the standard for currency. The Sumerians used it as a standard of measure. When the Aryans left the Iranian plateau to conquer India, they brought *djavas* (barley), the grain of soldiers, with them. Over the centuries, soldiers continued to consume barley to gain strength. The gladiators of ancient Rome ate so much of it that they were called *hordearii,* after the Latin name for barley, *hordeum.* Greek Olympians used it as a primary training food.

Evidence of barley has been unearthed from the carbonized remains of the Stone Age Swiss Lake dwellers, making it a dominant cereal in Neolithic and Bronze Age Europe. It traveled along the ancient trade routes to Nepal, Tibet, China, and Japan. It was one of the first grains to be domesticated in China around 7000 B.C. Egyptian wall paintings from the Eleythya tomb as early as 1750 B.C. show harvesters below the Giza Plateau reaping crops of *djot,* barley, as well as millet. Heavily bearded barley was found in the tomb of King Tut as an offering to Osiris, god of agriculture, a symbol of resurrection. Unrisen barley bread is mentioned as daily bread in biblical writings, as the type of bread in the miracle of the loaves and fishes, and the manna of the Israelites.

In Great Britain during the Middle Ages, a grain of barley was known as a barleycorn, measuring about one-third of an inch. When malted, barley is the preferred cereal for making beer, the common man's drink known even to the Egyptians. The foam that forms on top of fermenting malt liquids, called barm, was commonly used for leavening breads until the cultivation of commercial yeasts in the nineteenth century. The Dutch and English settlers brought barley to the colonies in 1602, probably for the brewing of beer, a nutritious "liquid bread" beverage drunk instead of water.

The Tibetans, who grow and consume lots of barley, make a prayer wheel bread of barley flour and mix hot brewed tea with yak butter and barley flour to make their staple *tsampa* porridge dumplings. Norwegians are famous for their 100 percent barley breads and crackers; Finns bake the classic flatbread *rieska,* which looks like an oversized tortilla.

Today barley is the top crop in the Dakotas, Idaho, and eastern Washington, and is grown successfully from chilly Norway to the equatorial deserts and Tibetan highlands.

Barley has lots of healthy starch and fiber. It contains the alkaloid hordenine, a gentle diuretic. The concentration of protein is in the aleurone coating, removed during pearling, so the whole varieties with the hull intact are more nutritional. Barley is the best grain source for chromium.

Barley has a chewy texture and a mild, sweet flavor with a malty aftertaste. Crusts of barley breads bake up to a tan color and tend to harden as they cool, but the interiors are moist, with a tendency to crumble. Barley malt syrup, a sweet liquid made from the toasted and dried whole grain, is similar to molasses and serves as a wonderful sweetener for breads. When cooking barley, use whole barley; quick-cooking varieties tend to be mushy and also lack the bran and germ. The hull-less varieties developed at Montana State University, marketed under the name Nu-Barley—which includes waxy, hull-less Bronze Nugget and Black Buffalo from Western Trails—are more hearty than regular store-bought barley. Use a one-to-five ratio of barley flour to wheat flour, or one cup barley flour to five cups wheat flour, for a slightly bitter, moist bread that is excellent toasted. Bake barley breads at an oven temperature 25°F lower than regular wheat loaves to allow for more even baking.

Types of Products

Whole hulled barley is the entire kernel with just the hull (outer husk) removed. Also known as whole-grain barley, cleaned barley, pot barley, and Scotch barley.

Pearl barley refers to kernels that are steamed and polished by a special process to remove the tough outer hull, some germ, and the pericarp, leaving the starchy endosperm. Named because it looks like a little pearl seed, this is the type of barley commonly available—in fine, medium, and coarse sizes—in supermarkets.

Barley grits are cracked pieces of the kernel.

Rolled barley flakes are rolled and toasted pearl barley. Use like rolled oats.

Barley flour is finely ground pearl barley.

Barley flour mixed with wheat flour makes a wonderful sandwich loaf. (See photograph facing title page.)

Barley
Buttermilk Bread

Makes 2 round loaves

1¼ cups warm water (105° to 115°F)

1 tablespoon (1 package) active dry yeast

Pinch of light brown sugar or ½ teaspoon barley malt syrup

1 cup warm buttermilk (105° to 115°F)

2 tablespoons unsalted butter, melted

2 tablespoons packed light brown sugar or barley malt syrup

2½ teaspoons salt

1¾ cups barley flour

3½ to 4 cups bread flour

1. Pour ½ cup of the warm water into a small bowl. Sprinkle the yeast and sugar over the warm water. Stir to dissolve and let stand at room temperature until foamy, about 10 minutes.

2. In a large bowl using a whisk or in the bowl of a heavy-duty electric mixer fitted with the paddle attachment, combine the remaining ¾ cup warm water, buttermilk, butter, sugar, salt, and barley flour. Add the yeast mixture and beat hard for 2 minutes. Add the bread flour, ½ cup at a time, beating on low speed until a soft dough that just clears the sides of the bowl forms, switching to a wooden spoon when necessary if making by hand.

3. Turn the dough out onto a well-floured work surface and knead until firm, yet still soft and springy, 1 to 3 minutes for a machine-mixed dough and 3 to 5 minutes for a hand-mixed dough, dusting with flour only 1 tablespoon at a time, just enough as needed to prevent sticking. Do not add too much flour, or the dough will be hard and the bread will be dry. Place in a lightly greased deep container, turn once to coat the top, and cover with plastic wrap. Let rise at room temperature until double in bulk, 1½ to 2 hours.

4. Grease a baking sheet or line with parchment paper. Turn the dough out onto the work surface and divide into 2 equal portions. Form into round loaves and place on the prepared sheet. Cover loosely with plastic wrap and let rise until double in bulk, about 45 minutes.

5. About 20 minutes before baking, preheat an oven to 350°F and position a rack in the center of the oven.

6. Bake for 40 to 45 minutes, or until the loaves are brown and sound hollow when tapped with your finger. Remove from the baking sheet to cool on a rack.

Bread-Machine Barley Buttermilk Bread

1½-pound loaf

1 cup plus 3 tablespoons water

2 tablespoons unsalted butter, melted

2 tablespoons packed brown sugar

2½ cups bread flour

½ cup barley flour

⅓ cup dry buttermilk powder

3 teaspoons vital wheat gluten

1 teaspoon salt

1¾ teaspoons bread machine yeast

1-pound loaf

⅞ cup water

1½ tablespoons unsalted butter, melted

1½ tablespoons packed brown sugar

1⅔ cups bread flour

⅓ cup barley flour

¼ cup dry buttermilk powder

2 teaspoons vital wheat gluten

¾ teaspoon salt

1¼ teaspoons bread machine yeast

1. Place all of the ingredients in the pan according to the manufacturer's instructions. Set crust on medium and program for the basic bread cycle; press Start.

2. After the baking cycle ends, remove the bread from the pan, and place on a rack to cool to room temperature before slicing.

This is my basic berry muffin recipe, which I originally adapted from Our Daily Bread *by Stella Standard, published long before healthy breads became popular. Layering the berries keeps you from overworking the batter.*

Barley Blueberry Muffins

Makes 12 muffins

1½ cups fresh blueberries

2 to 4 tablespoons granulated sugar

6 tablespoons (¾ stick) unsalted butter, at room temperature

⅓ cup packed light brown sugar

2 large eggs

1 cup barley flour

1 cup unbleached all-purpose flour

1 tablespoon baking powder

½ teaspoon salt

1 cup whole milk

1 teaspoon pure vanilla extract

Cardamom Sugar

¼ cup sifted light brown sugar

1 teaspoon ground cardamom

1. Place the blueberries in a small bowl. Sprinkle with the granulated sugar to taste and let stand for 15 minutes.

2. Preheat an oven to 375°F and position a rack in the center of the oven. Grease 12 standard muffin cups.

3. In a bowl, cream the butter and brown sugar until smooth and fluffy. Add the eggs, one at a time, and beat until well mixed. In another bowl, combine the barley and all-purpose flours, baking powder, and salt. Add the dry ingredients to the creamed butter and sugar alternating with the milk and vanilla; stir with a large spatula just until moistened, using no more than 15 to 20 strokes. The batter will be lumpy.

4. Half fill each muffin cup with batter. Sprinkle with a thick layer of berries. Cover the berries with the remaining batter until just level with the top of the pan. Mix the sugar with the cardamom and sprinkle over the tops.

5. Bake until the tops are brown and feel dry and springy, and a cake tester inserted into the center comes out clean, 20 to 25 minutes. Let the muffins rest in the pan for 5 minutes before removing to a rack to cool.

Honey, cinnamon, and golden raisins result in a spicy-sweet bread. I also make this bread with chopped golden Calimyrna figs, which particularly complement the barley. The loaves are best served at room temperature.

Cinnamon-Raisin Barley Bread

Makes two 8-by-4-inch loaves

1 cup boiling water

1¼ cups rolled barley flakes

1 tablespoon salt

½ cup honey

4 tablespoons (½ stick) unsalted butter or margarine

½ cup warm water (105° to 115°F)

2 tablespoons (2 packages) active dry yeast

Pinch of sugar

1½ cups whole-wheat flour

1 tablespoon plus 1 teaspoon ground cinnamon

1 cup buttermilk

1¼ cups golden raisins

2 to 2½ cups bread flour

Rolled barley flakes, for sprinkling

1. In a large bowl using a whisk or in the bowl of a heavy-duty electric mixer fitted with the whisk attachment, combine the boiling water, 1¼ cups barley flakes, salt, honey, and butter. Mix until the butter melts. Let stand for about 20 minutes to cool to warm room temperature. The barley will swell and the mixture will thicken.

2. Pour the warm water into a small bowl or 1-cup liquid measuring cup. Sprinkle the yeast and sugar over the water. Stir to dissolve and let stand at room temperature until foamy, about 10 minutes.

3. Add the yeast mixture, whole-wheat flour, cinnamon, and buttermilk to the barley mixture. Beat hard until creamy, 1 minute. Add the raisins. Add the bread flour, ½ cup at a time, mixing on low speed until a soft, shaggy dough that just clears the sides of the bowl forms, switching to a wooden spoon when necessary if making by hand. The dough will be slightly sticky.

4. Turn the dough out onto a lightly floured work surface and knead until soft and springy, 1 to 3 minutes for a machine-mixed dough and 3 to 5 minutes for a hand-mixed dough, dusting with flour only 1 tablespoon at a time, just enough as needed to prevent sticking. The dough will be smooth and springy with

a nubby surface, but not dry. Place the dough in a lightly greased deep container, turn once to coat the top, and cover with plastic wrap. Let rise at room temperature until double in bulk, 2 to 2½ hours.

5. Grease two 8-by-4-inch loaf pans and sprinkle the bottom and sides with barley flakes. Turn the dough out onto a lightly floured work surface and divide into 2 equal portions. Pat each portion into a rectangle and roll into a loaf shape. Place the loaves, seam side down, in the prepared pans, and cover loosely with plastic wrap. Let rise until double in bulk or about 1 inch above the rims of the pans, 1 to 1½ hours.

6. About 20 minutes before baking, preheat an oven to 350°F and position a rack in the center of the oven.

7. Using a sharp knife, make 3 diagonal slashes no more than ¼ inch deep down the top of each loaf. Bake for 40 to 45 minutes, or until the tops are golden brown, the sides slightly contract from the pan, and the loaves sound hollow when tapped with your finger. A bamboo skewer inserted into the center should come out clean. Remove the loaves from the pans to cool on a rack.

Scones are a traditional Scottish home-baked bread. Many old-country recipes for maslin scones call for a combination of barley, rye, and wheat flour. Barley flour is at its best in these orange-scented scones. They are crumbly and sweet with an addictive homey taste.

Orange Barley Scones with Cranberries and Walnuts

Makes 12 scones

1½ cups barley flour

1½ cups unbleached all-purpose flour

½ cup sugar

2½ teaspoons baking powder

½ teaspoon salt

½ teaspoon freshly ground nutmeg

6 tablespoons (¾ stick) cold unsalted butter, cut into pieces

Grated zest of 1 orange

1 cup whole fresh cranberries

¼ cup chopped walnuts

2 large eggs

About 1 cup cold milk or half-and-half

1. Preheat an oven to 400°F and position a rack in the center of the oven. Line a baking sheet with parchment paper.

2. In a bowl, combine the barley and all-purpose flours, sugar, baking powder, salt, and nutmeg. Cut in the butter with a fork or 2 knives until the mixture resembles coarse crumbs. Add the orange zest, cranberries, and walnuts, and toss to distribute. Add the eggs and milk and stir until a sticky shaggy dough forms.

3. Turn the dough out onto a lightly floured work surface and knead gently just until the dough comes together into a ball, about 6 times. Divide the dough into 2 equal portions. Pat each portion into an 8-inch round. Using a knife, cut each round into 6 wedge shapes. Place the scones about 1 inch apart on the prepared sheet.

4. Bake until crusty and golden brown, 15 to 20 minutes. The scones are best served immediately.

Buckwheat

Buckwheat is technically not a grain, but the hardy fruit of the *Fagopyrum* genus, a shallow-rooted, red-stemmed annual bush related to rhubarb and sorrel. It is a branching plant with smooth triangular heart-shaped leaves and a fetching corolla of papery-textured white blossoms that yield the three-cornered pyramidal cream-colored seed. It is an extremely hardy commercial crop requiring no field chemicals, a boon to the organic foods industry. Honeybees love the flowers and produce a rich, aromatic honey.

Buckwheat originated primarily in the shores surrounding the unique Lake Baikal area in Siberia, the planet's oldest and deepest freshwater lake, home to hundreds of plant species found nowhere else. According to the writings of ancient historians such as Herodotus and Pliny, buckwheat was the last of the grains to be cultivated, less than two thousand years ago. It first appeared in Manchuria and the Himalayan highlands, then became a staple throughout mainland Asia and later, in Japanese and Indian diets. The Chinese have grown a perennial species for over one thousand years. The Hindus still eat buckwheat on fast days. The Japanese steam and dry the grain to make their famous *soba-kiri* noodles and a bread called *soba-neri*.

Buckwheat was introduced in the twelfth century to northern Europe overland from Russia into the Slavic states, and by way of Asia Minor into the Mediterranean through the maritime trade, although the ancient Phoenicians knew of it and ground it into a flour called *far.* Buckwheat is still referred to as *blé noir,* the black wheat, or *farine de sarrasin,* "Saracen grain," in France, Spain, and Italy, showing its association with Moslem culture. Buckwheat plantations readily sprang up in Germany, Poland, France, and Italy, countries settled by the Crusaders returning from fighting the Saracens in the Holy Land.

Buckwheat is featured extensively in the baking repertoires of Scandinavia, Eastern Europe, and Russia, areas of poor soil and less than temperate climates, and is a staple in Jewish cuisine. It came to the New World with Dutch settlers, primarily as animal fodder. Planted extensively in the Hudson River Valley of New York, it can be seen growing wild along northeastern turnpikes and is still an important cultivated crop in these states, especially since there often is not enough buckwheat to meet the demand.

Prime buckwheat land is found in Ohio, Maine, the Finger Lakes area of New York, Pennsylvania, Minnesota, and Canada. Some buckwheat is grown in western states, but it is earmarked for export to Japan. The fresh flour is available after harvest in early September.

Buckwheat is nutritionally similar to wheat: high in protein and all eight amino acids (especially lysine), and B vitamins (it has double the amount in wheat). These attributes make it a good dietary addition for vegetarians. It is exceptionally high in manganese, potassium, phosphorus, iron, calcium, and copper.

Buckwheat has a fine, grainy texture, and the hulls contain the strongest flavor and concentration of protein. Buckwheat can be intensely earthy flavored when roasted, but quite mild when prepared from raw hulled grain. The flavor is sometimes so assertive that buckwheat has the reputation as the "love-it-or-leave-it" grain. The strain grown in Europe (at this writing not available for purchase in this country) has a rather mild taste, distinctly different from the Japanese strain grown in the United States, which can be quite earthy and musky.

Buckwheat flour is naturally low in protein, which makes for a tender baked product with an assertive, musky, slightly bitter flavor. It contains a small amount of gluten. I find that a small proportion of the flour combined with wheat flour makes delicious light-textured bread with an almost violet color and dusky autumnal flavor. At most, use a one-to-five ratio of buckwheat flour to wheat flour, or one cup buckwheat flour to five cups wheat flour. The purple-gray color of the dough bakes into a hard, dark gray-brown crust. The more buckwheat flour used, the more compact the loaf will be. Buckwheat flour has a natural, and historic, love affair with apples and apple brandy. It is a favorite flour of sourdough enthusiasts, as the flavors are complementary.

Types of Products

Whole buckwheat groats are often stone-ground without the seeds having been cracked and are packaged as hulled groats, which are excellent as a hot breakfast cereal. Groats can be ivory to greenish ivory in color. They are used for sprouting and flour, cracked into coarse or fine grits, and cooked whole as an addition to doughs.

Buckwheat flour is available light or dark. The dark is the most assertive in flavor, depending on how much of the hull is ground. The light is a creamy beige and more delicate in flavor. I prefer the subtle mild flavor of the light flour.

Kasha, also known as brown buckwheat, is hulled factory-roasted buckwheat that comes in coarse, medium, and fine consistencies. In cooking, it is traditionally sealed with a beaten egg and then pan-roasted to prevent mushiness. It can be added to doughs.

Cream of buckwheat, a type of grits, is the finely cracked endosperm of hulled groats, marketed as a hot breakfast cereal like farina. It can be used interchangeably with other types of grits and for sprinkling like cornmeal and farina.

Mild whole buckwheat groats are cooked in milk just until chewy and then added to the dough to create a rich-textured, and unusual, whole-grain bread. This bread is perfect to serve in the winter with beef brisket or a thick turkey-vegetable soup.

Molasses Buckwheat Bread

Makes two 8-by-4-inch loaves

2 cups nonfat milk

1 cup whole buckwheat groats

1¼ cups warm water (105° to 115°F)

1½ tablespoons (scant 2 packages) active dry yeast

¼ cup packed light brown sugar

4 to 4½ cups bread flour

1½ cups white whole-wheat flour

½ cup medium rye flour

1 tablespoon salt

6 tablespoons (¾ stick) unsalted butter, melted

½ cup light molasses

2 tablespoons unsalted butter, melted, for brushing

1. Place the milk in a saucepan and bring to a boil. Add the groats, reduce the heat to a simmer, and cook for 15 minutes. Remove from heat and let stand for 5 minutes. Return to medium heat and cook for 5 minutes. Remove from heat and let stand for 15 minutes to cool slightly. The mixture will be soupy.

2. Meanwhile, pour the warm water into a small bowl. Sprinkle the yeast and a pinch of the brown sugar over the water and stir to dissolve. Let stand at room temperature until foamy, about 10 minutes.

3. In a large bowl using a whisk or in the bowl of a heavy-duty electric mixer fitted with the paddle attachment, combine 1 cup of the bread flour, the whole-wheat and rye flours, the remaining brown sugar, and the salt. Add the cooked buckwheat groats and milk, the 6 tablespoons butter, and the molasses. Beat hard until creamy, about 1 minute. Add the yeast mixture and beat well. Add the remaining bread flour, ½ cup at a time, mixing on low speed until a soft, shaggy dough that just clears the sides of the bowl forms, switching to a wooden spoon when necessary if making by hand.

4. Turn the dough out onto a lightly floured work surface and knead until the dough is soft, sticky, and

continued

elastic and holds its shape, 1 to 3 minutes for a machine-mixed dough and 4 to 7 minutes for a hand-mixed dough, dusting with flour only 1 tablespoon at a time, just enough as needed to prevent sticking. Place the dough in a lightly greased deep container, turn once to coat the top, and cover with plastic wrap. Let rise at room temperature until double in bulk, 1½ to 2 hours.

5. Grease the bottom and sides of two 8-by-4-inch loaf pans (I like to use terra-cotta pans). Turn the dough out onto a clean work surface and divide into 2 equal portions. Pat each portion into a rectangle and roll into a loaf shape. Place the loaves, seam side down, into the prepared pans. Cover loosely with plastic wrap and let rise again until the dough is puffy and about 1 inch above the rims of the pans, about 1 hour.

6. About 20 minutes before baking, preheat an oven to 350°F and position a rack in the center of the oven.

7. Brush the tops of the loaves with the 2 tablespoons melted butter. Using a sharp knife, make 3 pairs of opposing diagonal slashes no more than ¼ inch deep down the center of each loaf to form a herringbone design. Bake for 40 to 45 minutes, or until the tops are deep brown, the sides slightly contract from the pans, and the loaves sound hollow when tapped with your finger. Remove from the pans to cool on a rack.

A combination of buckwheat, white, and whole-wheat flours is enhanced with the strong spiciness of cinnamon and the buttery flavor of pecans to make a fine loaf with a light, moist texture. Slices of the bread are great toasted and also excellent served with Vermont cheddar or California chèvre.

Buckwheat Bread with Cinnamon and Pecans

Makes two 8-by-4-inch loaves

4 to 4½ cups bread flour

1¼ cups light buckwheat flour

¼ cup whole-wheat flour

½ cup dry buttermilk powder

1½ tablespoons ground cinnamon

1¼ tablespoons (1¼ packages) active dry yeast or
     1 tablespoon instant dry yeast

1 tablespoon salt

2 cups hot water (120°F)

⅓ cup walnut oil or unsalted butter, melted

⅓ cup pure maple syrup

¾ cup chopped pecans

1. In a large bowl using a whisk or in the bowl of a heavy-duty electric mixer fitted with the paddle attachment, combine 1 cup of the bread flour, the buckwheat and whole-wheat flours, buttermilk powder, cinnamon, yeast, and salt. Add the hot water. Beat hard until creamy, about 1 minute. Add the walnut oil, maple syrup, and pecans and beat for 1 minute longer. Add the remaining bread flour, ½ cup at a time, mixing on low speed until a soft, shaggy dough that just clears the sides of the bowl forms, switching to a wooden spoon when necessary if making by hand. The dough will be slightly stiff and very sticky.

2. Turn the dough out onto a lightly floured work surface and knead until the dough is soft, sticky, and elastic and holds its shape, 1 to 3 minutes for a machine-mixed dough and 3 to 6 minutes for a hand-mixed dough, dusting with flour only 1 tablespoon at a time, just enough as needed to prevent sticking. Place in a lightly greased deep container, turn once to coat the top, and cover with plastic wrap. Let rise at room temperature until double in bulk, 1½ to 2 hours.

3. Grease the bottom and sides of two 8-by-4-inch loaf pans (I like to use terra-cotta pans). Turn the dough out onto a clean work surface and divide into 2 equal portions. Pat each portion into a rectangle and roll into a loaf shape. Place the loaves, seam side down, into the prepared pans. Cover loosely with plastic wrap and let rise until the dough is puffy and about 1 inch above the rims of the pans, about 1 hour.

4. About 20 minutes before baking, preheat an oven to 350°F and position a rack in the center of the oven.

5. Using a sharp knife, make 3 diagonal slashes no more than ¼ inch deep down the top center of each loaf. Bake for 35 to 40 minutes, or until the tops are deep brown, the sides slightly contract from the pan, and the loaves sound hollow when tapped with your finger. Remove the loaves from the pans to cool on a rack.

Bread-Machine Buckwheat Bread with Cinnamon and Pecans

1½-pound loaf

1 cup plus 2 tablespoons water

⅓ cup pure maple syrup

3 tablespoons walnut oil or unsalted butter, melted

¼ cup dry buttermilk powder

1¾ cups bread flour

1 cup light buckwheat flour

¼ cup whole-wheat flour

4 teaspoons vital wheat gluten

1½ teaspoon salt

2½ teaspoons ground cinnamon

2 teaspoons bread machine yeast

½ cup chopped pecans

1-pound loaf

¾ cup water

¼ cup pure maple syrup

2 tablespoons walnut oil or unsalted butter, melted

3 tablespoons dry buttermilk powder

1 cup plus 3 tablespoons bread flour

⅔ cup light buckwheat flour

3 tablespoons whole-wheat flour

3 teaspoons vital wheat gluten

1 teaspoon salt

1¾ teaspoons ground cinnamon

1½ teaspoons bread machine yeast

⅓ cup chopped pecans

1. Place all the ingredients, except the pecans, in the pan according to the manufacturer's instructions. Set crust on medium and program for the sweet bread cycle or fruit and nut cycle; press Start. At the beep, add the fruits at midcycle; if using the sweet bread cycle, mix all the ingredients together.

2. After the baking cycle ends, remove the bread from the pan and place on a rack to cool to room temperature before slicing.

In the film Babette's Feast, *a single giant blini, one half covered with thick cream, the other with black caviar, was served as a first course. The pancake was eaten with great reverence and gustatory appreciation. For a similar feast, serve these blini topped with low-fat sour cream and a teaspoonful of iced caviar or strips of lox.*

Buckwheat Blini

Makes about twenty 3- to 4-inch blini

1¾ cups unbleached all-purpose flour

1 cup light buckwheat flour

2 teaspoons active dry yeast or instant yeast

2 tablespoons sugar

Pinch of salt

3 large eggs

2¾ cups warm milk (105° to 115°F)

⅓ cup unsalted butter, melted, plus butter for coating pan

1 to 2 cups low-fat sour cream

3 to 4 ounces golden, red, or black caviar or 6 to 8 ounces lox, thinly sliced

1. In a bowl, combine the all-purpose and buckwheat flours, yeast, sugar, and salt. Make a well in the center and add the eggs. Using a whisk or immersion blender on low speed, slowly mix in the warm milk and ⅓ cup melted butter until well blended; beat 1 minute and scrape down the sides of the bowl. Cover with plastic wrap and let stand at warm room temperature until double in bulk, about 1 hour.

2. Preheat an oven to 200°F. In a large frying pan or griddle over medium heat, melt some butter and brush lightly over the entire surface. Stir down the batter. Drop the batter by large heaping spoonfuls (I use a large spoon that is about 3 tablespoons) onto the hot surface. Cook until the bottom is golden brown and bubbles form on the surface, about 1 minute. Turn once. The second side will take about 30 seconds to cook. Keep warm in the oven until ready to serve. Or stack on a layer of paper towels to cool, cover loosely with plastic wrap, let stand up to 6 hours, and serve at room temperature. Stack 2 blini on each plate, top with a heaping tablespoon of sour cream, then with 1 teaspoon caviar or several slices of lox.

Ti Couz—which means "the old house" in Gaelic—is a popular San Francisco crêperie bretonne owned and run by Sylvie Le Mer, who was born and raised in lower Brittany. The savory buckwheat crêpes, known as krampouz, are traditional in this area of France. The traditional accompaniment is a good dry or sweet cider served in a ceramic bowl.

Ti Couz Buckwheat Crêpes

Makes about twenty-four 14- or 16-inch crêpes

9 cups water

3 cups milk

1 large egg

4 tablespoons (½ stick) unsalted butter, melted

2¾ cups whole-wheat flour

1⅔ cups unbleached all-purpose flour

1¼ cups light buckwheat flour

2 teaspoons salt

About ½ cup vegetable shortening, for coating pan

Unsalted butter or Breton Herb Butter
(recipe follows)

1. In a large ceramic bowl using a large whisk or in a large food processor fitted with the metal blade, combine the water, milk, egg, melted butter, whole-wheat, all-purpose, and buckwheat flours, and salt. Beat well until creamy, about 30 seconds. The batter will be the consistency of heavy cream. Cover and let stand at room temperature for about 1 hour. The batter can also be covered and refrigerated for up to 24 hours and brought to room temperature before cooking.

2. Assemble everything you will need for cooking the crêpes. Spread out a large clean kitchen towel on which to lay the finished crêpes after baking. Set out a measuring cup or a 6-ounce capacity ladle for the batter, a wide spatula for spreading the batters, and a long spatula for flipping the crêpes. Have ready a piece of paper towel for scooping out the shortening and greasing the hot pan.

3. Heat a 14- or 16-inch sauté pan or heavy paella pan over medium-high heat. Sprinkle the pan with a few drops of water. If the water sizzles, the pan is ready. Coat the pan lightly with shortening. Stir the batter. With one hand, ladle ⅔ cup batter onto the left side of the pan and, using the spatula, immediately pull the batter from left to right in a clockwise motion, spreading it in little strokes. (If you are left-handed, work in

continued

the opposite direction.) Pull the batter back over itself to make a thicker pancake than a traditional crêpe. Do not tilt the pan. It will take a few crêpes to get the rhythm. Cook until the edges are light brown and lift slightly off the pan, about 1 minute. Slide the long spatula under the crêpe and turn carefully. Cook just until brown in spots but not crispy, about 1 minute longer. The crêpes should remain soft. Lift gently onto the towel. Continue to make the crêpes, stirring the batter and greasing the pan lightly before cooking.

4. Serve immediately with unsalted butter or Breton Herb Butter. Place 1 crêpe on each plate, spread with butter, and cut into wedges. Or let the crêpes cool and refrigerate in plastic wrap for up to 2 days or freeze for up to 1 month. Frozen crêpes must be brought to room temperature before using to avoid tearing.

Breton Herb Butter

Makes 1½ cups

 2 tablespoons loosely packed fresh parsley leaves

 2 tablespoons loosely packed snipped fresh chives

 2 tablespoons loosely packed fresh chervil

 2 tablespoons loosely packed fresh watercress leaves

 1 cup (2 sticks) salted butter, at room temperature, cut into pieces

 2 teaspoons fresh lemon juice

 1 large shallot, minced

Place the herbs in a blender or in a food processor fitted with the metal blade. Process until chopped. Add the butter, lemon juice, and shallot and process just until smooth and evenly combined. Or, chop the herbs by hand; combine in a small bowl with the butter, lemon juice, and shallots; and blend with a fork, scraping the sides of the bowl as needed. Pack the butter into a covered crock or form into a log wrapped in plastic. Herb butter keeps for 1 week in the refrigerator or for up to 3 months in the freezer.

Corn

The sturdy stalk of corn with its characteristic top tassel is the most familiar of all the members of the Gramineae family. The annual plant contains alternating thick spikes, called ears, that jut out of the thick stem. The kernels that develop on the ears inside the green husks are delicious edible seeds. Different varieties are classified by the starchy inside texture: dent, flint, flour, pop, sweet, and waxy. The kernels are ground into a wide range of meals after the oil has been extracted.

Corn has been called everything from Turkish corn to Asiatic corn because it was thought to have been introduced by the invading Turks from Asia to Europe in the Middle Ages. The new grain was, in fact, one of the oldest ever cultivated. Although it originated in the tropics, corn now successfully grows from the Yukon to Tierra del Fuego, from the desert of the Southwest to the jungle of the Amazon basin.

While modern corn has become so highly domesticated that it is often referred to as a "biological monstrosity," the beginnings of the grain are quite controversial and the subject of much conjecture. A wild perennial grass named *teosinte,* the probable ancestor of the corn we know today, was transformed between eight thousand and fifteen thousand years ago into a primitive domesticated corn plant by human design. Since corn cannot set its own seed, humans must remove the kernels and plant seedlings. In nature, corn would have been extinct long ago, because it produces densely cluttered seedlings that choke each other to death by competing for nutrition and water. Corn, as we know it, is truly a product of the mutual dependence of man and nature, and a direct link to the agrarian past.

Beginning about 1500 B.C., corn traveled north-south from the Mexico hub by three main corridors. Along the Sierra Madre north-south corridor, from the Rockies to Colombia and Peru, corn adapted to the chilly highlands. The tropical route to Sonora and southern Arizona produced today's heat- and drought-resistant crops. An eastern corridor along the north-eastern United States resulted in corn that became the base for hybridized dents from the temperate corn belt in the 1920s—the commercial crop known for the dimple on top of each kernel. A fourth corridor opened a thousand years later into the humid, tropical climates of Florida, Virginia, and Louisiana, probably by sea from Cuba and the Caribbean. By the time the Pilgrims landed on the New England coast and were fashioning crude breads from corn that had a crimson red inner core, corn was already grown in over a thousand pure strains on this continent.

Columbus brought the first sample of maize from the Caribbean islands to Spain in the late 1500s. He described the heavy-stalked *mahiz,* the "stuff of life," in his diary as "good tasting, and all the people in this land live on it." Within a few hundred years, Indian corn would take its place as one of the three most important cereals of the world, a profound agricultural gift from the New World to the Old.

Italy was the first European country to plant cornfields. Enough was grown of the new grain to supply the entire Mediterranean basin. The Venetians traded it to the Turks, for whom it became the national grain due to its appearance—it reminded the Muslims of a wound turban. The curve of the sickle and sword, on the edict of Mohammed and the Koran, became the symbol of the maize harvest to the nomadic sons of the crescent moon. The maize of the Near East gained the name Turkish corn. Wherever they went, the Turks left the maize grain behind—the Euphrates River Valley, Hungary, Yugoslavia, the Balkans. Portuguese traders took it to Africa and India. Ferdinand Magellan brought Indian corn with him to Indonesia, the Philippines, and Java. It reached New Zealand, Japan, and China by the sixteenth century, and followed the Ottomans to Rumania. In the 1600s, an Italian farmer was asked to cultivate Turkish corn for Rumanian royalty; the delicious results ended up being the variety grown today in northern Italy.

Corn is generally low in protein, vitamins, and minerals, but has some B vitamins, iron, and calcium. It is the only grain to contain vitamin A in the form of beta-carotene. Stone-ground meals, which are not heated and crushed, are high in fiber, riboflavin, niacin, and iron.

Baked goods made with cornmeal are crumbly in texture and a bit gritty, with a characteristic pale yellow color; the more cornmeal or the coarser the grind, the more crumbly the baked product. The flavor of corn is delightfully delicate and sweet. Quick breads made with corn—johnnycakes, corn pones, corn sticks, corn muffins, and skillet corn breads—bake into crumbly breads with a sandy texture.

Types of Products

Cornmeal refers to whole kernels of unparched yellow or white dent corn ground into a meal. It is available in fine, medium, or coarse grinds, stone-ground or degerminated (with the germ removed for longer shelf life). Yellow and white cornmeals can be used interchangeably. Blue corn meal comes in shades from gray to black, characteristic of its high lysine and iron content. Red cornmeal is a bit harder to find.

Polenta is coarse-ground hulled and degermed cornmeal. It comes in coarse or fine grinds, regular or instant.

Corn grits are cracked pieces of whole dried degerminated yellow or white corn, considered the coarsest-grind cornmeal, and are available in fine,

medium, or coarse grinds. Stone-ground grits contain bits of bran and germ. Corn grits are sometimes called hominy grits, but are not ground from hominy.

Corn bran is the outer husk of the whole grain. Use it like oat or wheat bran.

Corn flour is finely ground whole or degermed kernels of corn. Creamy to a soft canary in color, it is the finest grind of cornmeal and is rich in oil. Do not confuse with cornstarch.

Whole hominy is dried corn that has been cooked in an alkali solution to soften and loosen the hulls. When the skins pop off, the remaining starchy kernels become chewy in texture and earthy in flavor, as well as easy to digest. Hominy is available dried, fresh, and canned. Whole canned hominy is an excellent addition to breads, giving a wonderful moist texture and a pleasant, slightly tangy smell and taste.

Masa harina is available stone-ground from white, blue, or yellow hominy. Though it is the product specifically used for making tortillas, it can be used as an ingredient in breads when mixed with bread flour, as well as in quick corn breads, pancakes, and unique biscuits. Blue corn masa harina is usually mixed with a small percentage of white or yellow masa harina to help hold the tortillas together. Coarse grinds are used for tamales, fine grinds for tortillas.

Dried corn husks, or *hojas de maiz,* from Mexican field or sweet corn, are the traditional wrappings for steamed tamales or are formed into cooking baskets, but are also wonderful for cradling muffins and yeast breads. They contribute a delicate corn flavor. Rinse and remove the silks before soaking in warm water about 1 hour, or until pliable, for easiest handling. Corn husks are inedible.

These muffins would be made with yellow johnnycake meal in New England, white cornmeal in the South and Texas, and blue or red cornmeal in the Southwest. There is no real difference in how they bake if you use a finely ground meal, but the appearance of the final product will vary. Stone-ground cornmeal of any color will give the brightest taste. These muffins are ideal if you are on a dairy- or sugar-restricted diet.

Nondairy Corn Bread Muffins

Makes 12 muffins

1½ cups unbleached all-purpose flour

1½ cups fine-grind yellow, blue, white, or red cornmeal, preferably stone-ground

4 teaspoons baking powder

½ teaspoon salt

2 large eggs

¼ cup honey

1½ cups plain soy milk

½ cup corn oil

1. Grease 12 standard muffin cups. Preheat an oven to 375°F and position a rack in the center of the oven.

2. In a bowl, combine the flour, cornmeal, baking powder, and salt. In another bowl, combine the eggs, honey, soy milk, and oil with a whisk. Add to the dry ingredients and stir just until moistened. Spoon the batter into the prepared muffin cups until level with the tops.

3. Bake for 20 to 24 minutes, or until the tops are springy to the touch and a cake tester inserted into the center comes out clean. Let stand in the pan for 5 minutes before removing to cool on a rack.

Cornmeal mush is the base for American-style loaf breads. This combination of cornmeal, wheat, and molasses has been a New England favorite since colonial days. Butter replaces the traditional bacon fat.

Whole-Wheat New England Anadama Bread

Makes two 8-by-4-inch loaves

½ cup medium-grind yellow cornmeal, preferably stone-ground, plus cornmeal for sprinkling

1¾ cups boiling water

½ cup light or dark molasses

2 tablespoons unsalted butter, at room temperature

⅔ cup warm water (105° to 115°F)

1 tablespoon (1 package) active dry yeast

2½ to 3 cups bread flour

Pinch of sugar

2 cups coarse-grind whole-wheat flour

2 teaspoons salt

1. In a large bowl using a whisk or in the bowl of a heavy-duty electric mixer fitted with the paddle attachment, combine the ½ cup cornmeal and the boiling water. Stir until well mixed. Add the molasses and butter; stir until the butter is melted. Let cool until warm, about 1 hour.

2. Pour the warm water into a small bowl. Sprinkle the yeast, 1 tablespoon of the bread flour, and the sugar over the warm water. Stir to dissolve and let stand until foamy, about 10 minutes.

3. Add the yeast mixture, whole-wheat flour, and salt to the cornmeal mixture. Beat for 2 minutes. Add the remaining bread flour, ½ cup at a time, mixing on low speed until a soft dough that just clears the sides of the bowl forms, about 2 minutes. Switch to a wooden spoon when necessary if making by hand.

4. Turn the dough out onto a lightly floured work surface and knead until soft and smooth with a grainy texture, 1 to 2 minutes for a machine-mixed dough and 3 to 4 minutes for a hand-mixed dough, dusting with flour only 1 tablespoon at a time, just enough as needed to prevent sticking. Place in a lightly greased

deep container, turn once to coat the top, and cover with plastic wrap. Let rise at room temperature until double in bulk, about 1½ hours.

5. Lightly grease two 8-by-4-inch loaf pans and sprinkle with cornmeal. Turn the dough out onto the work surface and divide into 2 equal portions. Form into rectangular loaves and pinch the seams to seal. Place, seam side down, in the prepared pans. Cover loosely with plastic wrap and let rise until double in bulk, or 1 inch above the rims of the pans, about 50 minutes.

6. About 20 minutes before baking, preheat an oven to 350°F and position a rack in the center of the oven.

7. Bake for 45 to 50 minutes, or until the tops are brown and the loaves sound hollow when tapped with your finger. Remove from the pans to cool on a rack.

Bread-Machine Whole-Wheat New England Anadama Bread

1. Place all of the ingredients in the pan according to the manufacturer's instructions. Set crust on medium and program for the basic or whole-wheat bread cycle; press Start.

2. After the baking cycle ends, remove the bread from the pan and place on a rack to cool to room temperature.

1½-pound loaf

1¼ cups water

¼ cup molasses

1½ tablespoons unsalted butter, melted

2 cups bread flour

1 cup whole-wheat flour

⅓ cup medium-grind yellow cornmeal

4 teaspoons vital wheat gluten

1 teaspoon salt

1¾ teaspoons bread machine yeast

1-pound loaf

¾ cup water

3 tablespoons molasses

1 tablespoon unsalted butter, melted

1¼ cups bread flour

¾ cups whole-wheat flour

¼ cup medium-grind yellow cornmeal

3 teaspoons vital wheat gluten

¾ teaspoon salt

1¼ teaspoons bread machine yeast

These crêpes are actually thin pancakes suitable for filling with beans, meat, or vegetables and topping with sauce. Easier to make than tortillas, they are perfect for baked casserole dishes such as enchiladas. Add a few teaspoons of chili powder or chopped fresh herbs to the batter for spicy crêpes. You can substitute finely ground yellow, white, or red cornmeal.

Blue Corn Crêpes

Makes 14 crêpes

¾ cup fine-grind blue cornmeal

¼ cup unbleached all-purpose flour

¼ teaspoon salt

3 large eggs

1½ tablespoons corn or vegetable oil

1 cup milk

Melted butter for coating pan

1. In a bowl, combine the cornmeal, flour, salt, eggs, oil, and milk with a whisk. Beat hard for 15 seconds. The batter can also be mixed with an immersion blender or in a food processor fitted with the metal blade. Cover and place in the refrigerator for at least 30 minutes or for up to 24 hours.

2. Heat a shallow 6- to 7-inch nonstick or crêpe pan over high heat. When hot, brush lightly with butter. Pour in 2 tablespoons batter, tilting and rotating the pan quickly to coat the entire surface. Cook for 1 minute, or until the top is almost dry. Loosen the edge with a spatula, turn, and cook for about 15 seconds. Invert the pan to release the crêpe onto a clean kitchen towel. The crêpes can be refrigerated for 2 days or frozen for up to 1 month.

There are never enough recipes for summer squash, a bountiful home garden vegetable. Casserole breads like this one are raised by yeast but do not have to be kneaded. This moist-textured, light loaf has a hint of cheese. Serve it sliced, or cut into wedges, with sweet butter. The bread is delicious with main-dish salads, thick stews, and soups such as clam chowder.

Zucchini Cornmeal Bread

Makes 1 loaf

½ cup warm water (105° to 115°F)

1 tablespoon (1 package) active dry yeast

1 tablespoon sugar

½ cup warm milk (105° to 115°F)

1 large egg

1¼ teaspoons salt

3 tablespoons olive oil

¼ cup shredded Parmesan or Asiago cheese

½ cup fine-grind yellow or blue cornmeal

3 cups bread flour

1¼ cups coarsely grated unpeeled zucchini

1. Pour the warm water into a small bowl or 1-cup liquid measuring cup. Sprinkle the yeast and a pinch of the sugar over the water. Stir to dissolve and let stand until foamy, about 10 minutes.

2. In a large bowl using a whisk or in the bowl of a heavy-duty electric mixer fitted with the paddle attachment, combine the remaining sugar, warm milk, egg, salt, oil, cheese, cornmeal, and 1½ cups of the bread flour. Beat until smooth. Add the yeast mixture, zucchini, and remaining bread flour, ½ cup at a time, beating vigorously, about 2 minutes. The batter will be sticky. Scrape down the sides of the bowl and cover with plastic wrap. Let rise at room temperature until double in bulk, about 1½ hours.

3. Generously grease the bottom and sides of an 8-inch springform pan or 2-quart casserole or soufflé dish. Scrape the batter into the pan and press with wet fingers to the edges of the pan. Cover loosely with plastic wrap and let rise until double in bulk, about 50 minutes.

4. About 20 minutes before baking, preheat an oven to 375°F and position a rack in the center of the oven.

5. Bake for 40 to 45 minutes, or until the top is crusty brown, the bread sounds hollow when tapped with your finger, and a cake tester inserted into the center comes out clean. Run a sharp knife around the sides of the pan and carefully turn the bread onto a rack. Invert and cool right side up.

Enjoy the tortilla taste of masa harina de maiz, *fine white cornmeal ground from dried hominy, in these biscuits. They are delicate, with a fluffy interior, good with butter for dinner or with jam for breakfast.*

Masa Biscuits

Makes 12 biscuits

3 cups unbleached all-purpose flour, plus
    2 tablespoons for sprinkling

2 tablespoons white cornmeal, for sprinkling

1 cup yellow or white masa harina

2 tablespoons baking powder

1 teaspoon cream of tartar

1 teaspoon salt

¾ cup (1½ sticks) chilled unsalted butter,
    cut into pieces

1½ cups buttermilk

1. Preheat an oven to 425°F and position a rack in the center of the oven. Grease a baking sheet or line with parchment paper and sprinkle with the 2 tablespoons flour and cornmeal.

2. In a large bowl, combine the 3 cups flour, masa harina, baking powder, cream of tartar, and salt. Cut in the butter with a pastry blender or 2 knives until the mixture resembles coarse crumbs and no large chunks of butter remain. Add the buttermilk and stir just until all the ingredients are moistened. The dough will be slightly shaggy, but not sticky.

3. Turn the dough out onto a lightly floured work surface and knead gently about 10 times, or just until it holds together. Roll or pat out the dough into a 1-inch-thick rectangle. Take care not to add too much flour or the biscuits will be tough. Cut with a sharp knife or pastry wheel into 12 equal squares and place ½ inch apart on the prepared sheet.

4. Bake for 15 to 18 minutes, or until golden brown. Let stand for 3 or 4 minutes and serve hot.

Millet

The prince of the grain world, millet is also affectionately dubbed "father millet," as it is the first known grain to have been domesticated. The term refers to a very large and confusing variety of plants with small seeds. The commonly known millet is part of the true grain family, one of the temperate millets called *proso*—the small, glossy, round seeds that look like miniature pearls.

In North America, proso millet is sadly used mostly for livestock and birdseed; the only difference between the millet for humans and that for birdseed is that the millet for birds is not hulled. Millet is more popular in other countries, for making unfermented breads like *injera* in Ethiopia and *roti* in India, beer and a thick or thin porridge in Russia, and for steaming like couscous in Northern Africa.

Grain millet is native to the northern provinces of China, with datings to 2800 B.C. It is mentioned as the "holy plant" in the Fan Shen-Chiu Shu agricultural tablets. It was grown in the fertile loess soil of river basins similar to the Tigrus-Euphrates and Nile valleys. Millet is a cornerstone in the five sacred crops of China along with soy, rice, wheat, and barley. Wild millet was being gathered around 7000 B.C. in Japan. It is still the grain of choice in Central Asia. The Stone Age Swiss Lake dwellers were making crude breads, baked in ashes, of crushed wild millet, rye, barley, oats, and caraway.

Millet is a staple in the diet of the Hunzas of the Himalayas and has the reputation as the grain to eat for longevity. It spread to ancient India and also to Egypt, Assyria, Babylonia, and Africa. The Greek historian Herodotus wrote of the bread being eaten in the ancient world and the cultivation of grains during his journeys into the Near East in the fifth century B.C. He tells of millet growing profusely in the hanging gardens of Babylon and enticingly sprouted as weeds between the legs of the Colossus of Rhodes.

Although proso millet is usually what you will get in the natural-foods store, heirloom varieties grown in small plots are sometimes available, and Japanese varieties are imported for the macrobiotic community. The harvest is in early fall, and the new crop of millet is especially sweet and delicate.

Millet has lots of amino acids, a trace of fat, and plenty of carbohydrates. Millet contains lysine, B vitamins, magnesium, copper, and thiamine. It is the only grain that becomes alkaline when cooked, so it is easily digested. Even though millet is hulled, all of the nutrition inherent in the grain is left intact.

Millet has a slightly sweet, delicate taste. It can become bitter and sticky when steamed raw; dry toast or sauté it first in oil before steaming. Toasted millet has a nutty taste. Steamed millet is bright golden, fluffy, and soft. Millet can be added whole to breads and retains a delightful crunchy texture. Often millet is soaked in hot water to soften slightly before being added to bread doughs. Millet is one of the key ingredients in seven- and nine-grain blends and in Essene and Ezekiel sprouted wheat breads.

Use a one-to-five ratio of millet flour to wheat flour, or a scant one cup millet flour to five cups wheat flour. Millet flour makes a fine-grained creamy-colored loaf with a soft crumb. Crusts bake to a tan color and tend to get denser in texture as they cool.

Types of Products

Raw whole millet is the hulled whole grain.

Millet grits or millet meal is coarsely ground millet. It is a great breakfast porridge, very similar in texture to couscous.

Millet flour is the finely ground whole grain.

One of the most popular breads I make, these loaves have the mild nuttiness of sunflower seeds, the crunch of golden millet, and the moist sweetness of whole-wheat flour. Use the finest grind of whole-wheat flour you can obtain. If you find raw whole millet too tough, soak it in warm water for 1 hour and drain before adding to the dough. The loaves are best served slightly warm or at room temperature.

Sunflower Millet Health Bread

Makes two 8-by-4-inch loaves

1⅓ cups warm water (105° to 115°F)

1¼ tablespoons (1½ packages) active dry yeast

Pinch of sugar

1 cup warm evaporated milk (105° to 115°F), undiluted

¼ cup honey

1 cup raw sunflower seeds

1 cup raw whole millet

4½ cups fine-grind whole-wheat flour

3 tablespoons sunflower seed oil

1 tablespoon salt

1½ to 2 cups bread flour

2 tablespoons butter or margarine, melted, for brushing

1. Pour ⅓ cup of the warm water into a small bowl or 1-cup liquid measuring cup. Sprinkle the yeast and sugar over the water. Stir to dissolve and let stand at room temperature until foamy, about 10 minutes.

2. In a large bowl using a whisk or in the bowl of a heavy-duty electric mixer fitted with the paddle attachment, combine the remaining water, milk, honey, sunflower seeds, millet, and 2 cups of the whole-wheat flour. Beat hard for about 2 minutes. Stir in the yeast mixture. Cover and let rest 30 minutes; the sponge will be puffy.

3. Add the oil, salt, and remaining whole-wheat flour, ½ cup at a time, beating on low speed for 1 minute or until smooth. Add the bread flour, ¼ cup at a time, mixing on low speed until a soft, shaggy dough that just clears the sides of the bowl forms, switching to a wooden spoon when necessary if making by hand.

4. Turn the dough out onto a lightly floured work surface and knead until smooth, soft, and springy, 1 to 3 minutes for a machine-mixed dough and 3 to 5 minutes for a hand-mixed dough, dusting with flour only 1 tablespoon at a time, just enough as needed to prevent sticking. Do not add too much flour or the loaves will be dry and crumbly. Place in a lightly greased deep container, turn once to coat the top, and cover with plastic wrap. Let rise at room temperature until double in bulk, 2 to 2½ hours. Do not allow to rise any higher, or it may collapse and bake into a flat loaf.

5. Lightly grease the bottom and sides of two 8-by-4-inch loaf pans. Turn the dough out onto a lightly floured work surface and divide into 2 equal portions. Pat each into a rectangle and roll into a loaf shape. Place in the prepared pans, seam side down. Cover loosely with plastic wrap and let rise until the dough is almost double in bulk and about 1 inch above the rims of the pans, about 50 minutes.

6. About 20 minutes before baking, preheat an oven to 375°F and position a rack in the center of the oven.

7. Brush the tops with butter. Bake for 35 to 40 minutes, or until the tops are golden brown, the sides slightly contract from the pans, and the loaves sound hollow when tapped with your finger. Remove from the pans to a rack.

This is my version of a bread machine recipe developed by food writer Narsai David, one of the first professionals to give the electronic kneading and baking machine his approval.

Bread-Machine Buckwheat-Millet Bread

1½-pound loaf

1 cup water

2 tablespoons unsalted butter, melted

3 tablespoons packed brown sugar

2⅓ cups bread flour

⅓ cup buckwheat flour

⅓ cup raw whole millet

¼ cup dry buttermilk powder

4 teaspoons vital wheat gluten

1 teaspoon salt

1¾ teaspoons bread machine yeast

1-pound loaf

¾ cup water

1½ tablespoons unsalted butter, melted

2 tablespoons packed brown sugar

1½ cups bread flour

¼ cup buckwheat flour

¼ cup raw whole millet

3 tablespoons dry buttermilk powder

3 teaspoons vital wheat gluten

¾ teaspoon salt

1¼ teaspoons bread machine yeast

1. Place all of the ingredients in the pan according to the manufacturer's instructions. Set crust on medium and program for the basic bread cycle; press Start.

2. After the baking cycle ends, remove the bread from the pan and place on a rack to cool to room temperature before slicing.

These soft, grain-rich buns are ideal for sandwiches and burgers, and for grilling, and they keep nicely in the freezer for up to two months. Millet and potatoes are a natural taste complement. I use Barbara's Mashed Potatoes, available at natural-food stores; although an instant product, they are just like freshly mashed potatoes. If you like, use a liquid egg substitute in place of the large eggs.

Multigrain Sandwich Buns

Makes nine 4-inch buns or twelve 3-inch buns

1 cup medium-grind whole-wheat flour

½ cup raw whole millet or millet grits

¼ cup sesame seeds

½ cup instant mashed potatoes

1 cup boiling water

1½ cups warm water (105° to 115°F)

1 tablespoon (1 package) active dry yeast

⅓ cup sugar

2 large eggs

2 tablespoons unsalted butter or margarine, melted

1 teaspoon salt

3 to 3½ cups bread flour

3 tablespoons sesame seeds, for sprinkling

1. Combine ½ cup of the whole-wheat flour, the millet, and the sesame seeds in a food processor fitted with the metal blade. Process until a coarse flour forms. In a small bowl, combine the instant mashed potatoes and boiling water; let cool to 105° to 115°F.

2. Pour ½ cup of the warm water into a small bowl or 1-cup liquid measuring cup. Sprinkle the yeast and a pinch of the sugar over the water. Stir to dissolve and let stand at room temperature until foamy, about 10 minutes.

3. In a large bowl using a whisk or in the bowl of a heavy-duty electric mixer fitted with the paddle attachment, combine the remaining warm water, remaining whole-wheat flour, sesame-millet flour, mashed potatoes, remaining sugar, 1 whole egg and 1 egg white (reserve the extra yolk for glazing), butter, and salt. Beat hard for about 2 minutes. Add the yeast mixture and beat for 2 minutes longer. Add the bread flour, ½ cup at a time, beating on low speed until a soft, shaggy dough that just clears the sides of the bowl forms, switching to a wooden spoon when necessary if making by hand.

continued

4. Turn the dough out onto a lightly floured work surface and knead until smooth, soft, and springy, 1 to 3 minutes for a machine-mixed dough and 3 to 5 minutes for a hand-mixed dough, dusting with flour only 1 tablespoon at a time, just enough as needed to prevent sticking. Place in a lightly greased deep container, turn once to coat the top, and cover with plastic wrap. Let rise at room temperature until double in bulk, about 1½ hours.

5. Line a baking sheet with parchment paper. Turn the dough out onto the work surface and divide into 9 or 12 equal portions, depending on the size roll you want. Form each into a tight round ball by rolling the dough with a cupped hand until smooth. Place, seam-side down at least 2 inches apart, on the prepared sheet. Flatten each ball into a 1-inch-thick disk with your palm. Cover loosely with plastic wrap and let rise until puffy, about 30 minutes.

6. About 20 minutes before baking, preheat an oven to 350°F and position a rack in the center of the oven.

7. Beat the reserved egg yolk with 1 teaspoon water. Brush on the tops of the buns and sprinkle with the sesame seeds. Bake until golden brown and firm to the touch, 20 to 25 minutes. Remove from the sheet to a rack to cool.

These simple, earthy muffins are studded with luscious red or golden raspberries. If your raspberries are very tart, sprinkle them with some of the sugar and let stand for fifteen minutes to sweeten them before folding into the batter.

Raspberry Millet Muffins

Makes 10 muffins

2 cups unbleached all-purpose flour

½ cup millet grits

⅔ cup sugar

2 teaspoons baking powder

½ teaspoon baking soda

¼ teaspoon salt

1 cup plus 2 tablespoons buttermilk

3 tablespoons unsalted butter or margarine, melted

2 large eggs

1½ cups fresh red or golden raspberries

1. Preheat an oven to 400°F and position a rack in the center of the oven. Grease 10 standard muffin cups.

2. In a large bowl, combine the flour, millet, sugar, baking powder, baking soda, and salt. In another bowl, combine the buttermilk, butter, and eggs and beat with a whisk or an electric mixer for 1 minute. Pour into the dry ingredients and stir with a large spatula just until moistened, using no more than 15 to 20 strokes. Gently fold in the raspberries, taking care not to break them up. The batter will be lumpy.

3. Spoon the batter into the prepared muffin cups until just level with the tops. Bake until the tops are browned and feel dry and springy, and a cake tester inserted into the center comes out clean, 20 to 25 minutes. Let the muffins rest in the pan for 5 minutes before removing to a rack to cool.

Oats

This annual grass that grows to five feet tall inhabits large expanses of grassy and uncultivated fields in the northern hemisphere. It has a beautiful spreading panicle bearing large, pendulous spikelets that fall open on a lazy, drooping stem.

The first evidence of wild oats, *Avena fatua*, appears in radiocarbon data gathered at the Franchthi Cave in Greece and is placed at 10,500 B.C. Another wild oat native to the hilly Tatary grasslands of Central Asia, it was especially favored for feeding the domesticated horse. Traces of wild oats date from the Iron Age in early Britain, and to this day, a type of black-bristled oats, *A. strigosa*, or 'Ceirch Llwyd,' grows in Wales where no other grain can.

Records show the Asian oat traveling along the early trade roots from Asia to the Middle East, Egypt, and Abyssinia around 2000 B.C. as livestock feed; wherever the horse traveled, oats followed. Originally despised by the Egyptians and Babylonians as diseased wheat and used extensively as animal fodder, it was a staple gruel known as *ptisane* for the very poor.

Oats appear in records of Aegean agriculture from around 600 B.C. as uncultivated "weeds of wheat," for the plant was a weed that appeared among wheat and barley crops, and was used extensively by the apothecary trade as medicine. The pre-Hellenic Eleusinian rites of Demeter offered an aphrodisiacal brew of oats and honey known as *kykeon* to initiates. The modern domesticated *A. sativa* descended from the Mediterranean wild oat, *A. sterilis*.

Before being known exclusively as an Anglo-Saxon porridge, oatmeal was the food of the foot soldiers from the time of Attila the Hun to the Crusades. The Roman legions brought their cultivated oats to the British Isles to make the flatbreads they carried into battle or hunting. The oat became a comforting staple grain in cold, harsh, moist temperate climates of the northern hemisphere. The English, Scots, Welsh, and Irish have many homey recipes that have been passed down over the generations for bakestone oatcakes and bannocks.

Cultivated oats came to America with the first British immigrants around 1600 and flourished in the cold wet climate of New England and Virginia. Oats were one of the first successful Old World crops at Plymouth colony. During the American Revolution, when flour was at a premium, fruit crisps and grunts were covered with a streusel topping of oats, sugar, and butter; this is still a favorite dessert topping today.

Wild oats were gathered off the Great Plains by Native Americans. The Scottish who settled in the northern Midwest planted oats in Minnesota, Wisconsin, South Dakota, Iowa, and central Canada, where they have flourished ever since (the best oatmeal bread recipes come from the Midwest). Oats are also grown in eastern Oregon, another area that was once home to wild oats.

Oats are very high in protein and contain concentrations of thiamine, pantothenic acid, iron, and zinc. Oat bran is rich in soluble fiber, as well as linoleic acid and vitamin E. Oats are often recommended as an alternate grain for people allergic to wheat, but if you are extremely sensitive to gluten or suffer from celiac disease, avoid this grain, as it contains traces of gluten.

Oats are sweet, earthy-flavored grains. Bread with oats has a pale cream–colored crust and interior. Oats can be ground into a coarse meal-like flour with a food processor suitable for bread making. Since oats have almost no gluten, oat products and oat flour must be mixed with white or whole-wheat flours for yeast breads. The more oats you use, the denser and more crumbly your bread will be, and every type of oat will give a different texture. At most use a one-to-three ratio of rolled oats to wheat flour, or two cups rolled oats to six cups wheat flour, and a one-to-five ratio of oat flour to wheat flour in light-textured yeast breads. You can use considerably more oat flour in quick breads.

Types of Products

Oat groats are whole hulled oats still containing the bran and germ. Use in breads as you would cooked rice or eat as a hot breakfast cereal.

Steel-cut oats, groats cut into small uniform chunks by steel bits, are used for making porridge. Scotch-cut or Irish-cut oats are cut by stone buhrs and make a creamier porridge. Finely ground oats are similar in texture to polenta.

Rolled oats are crushed and pressed from hulled and steamed oat groats by mechanical rollers into uniform flakes. They come in a variety of thicknesses, from medium to thick, to make the familiar breakfast cereal. The majority of bread recipes are made with rolled oats. Oatflakes are the thickest cut.

Quick-cooking oats are made from thin rolled groats that are slightly toasted during rolling so they cook fast. Quick-cooking or old-fashioned rolled oats can be used interchangeably in bread recipes: each has its own distinct flavor. Instant oats are rolled, pre-cooked, dried, and mixed with sugar, flavoring agents, salt, and wheat germ, and are not used in baking.

Oat flour is ground from the endosperm. It is a popular ingredient in baby foods and ready-to-eat breakfast cereals. Some health-food stores carry an oat flour ground from the whole groats. To make oat flour at home that is still a bit coarser than commercial oat flour but works fine in recipes, process 1¼ cups rolled oats in a food processor until finely textured. Makes 1 cup.

Oat bran is the outer layer of the groat and is combined with other flours to increase the fiber content of baked goods. It has a strong, sweet aroma.

This bread is made with the old-fashioned CoolRise® method developed by the Robin Hood Flour Company in the early 1970s. The dough is prepared one day and baked the next, a process that fits nicely into a busy schedule.

Overnight Sesame-Honey Oatmeal Bread

Makes two 9-by-5-inch loaves

2 cups boiling water

1 cup rolled oats

6 tablespoons (¾ stick) unsalted butter

⅔ cup warm water (105° to 115°F)

1½ tablespoons (scant 2 packages) active dry yeast

½ cup honey

6 to 6½ cups bread flour

⅓ cup sesame seeds

2½ teaspoons salt

1 tablespoon canola oil, for brushing

1 tablespoon honey mixed with 1 tablespoon hot water, for brushing

1. In a large bowl using a wooden spoon or in the bowl of a heavy-duty electric mixer fitted with the paddle attachment, combine the boiling water, oats, and butter. Stir to melt the butter and let stand until warm, about 30 minutes.

2. Pour the warm water into a small bowl or 1-cup liquid measuring cup. Sprinkle the yeast and drop a bit of the honey over water. Stir to dissolve and let stand at room temperature until foamy, about 10 minutes.

3. Add the remaining honey, 1 cup of the bread flour, the sesame seeds, and the salt to the warm oat mixture. Beat for 1 minute, or until smooth. Add the yeast mixture; beat for 1 minute longer. Add the remaining bread flour, ½ cup at a time, beating on low speed until a soft, shaggy dough that just clears the sides of the bowl forms, switching to a wooden spoon when necessary if making by hand.

4. Turn the dough out onto a lightly floured work surface and knead until smooth, soft, and springy, 1 to 2 minutes for a machine-mixed dough and 3 to 5 minutes for a hand-mixed dough, dusting with flour only 1 tablespoon at a time, just enough as needed to prevent

continued

sticking. Do not add too much flour or the dough will stiffen up. Cover with a clean towel and let rest on the work surface for 30 minutes.

5. Generously grease the bottom and sides of two 9-by-5-inch loaf pans (I use disposable aluminum or metal pans; they can take temperature changes best). Divide the dough into 2 equal portions. Pat each into a flat, fat oval and fold over to make a loaf with a thick folded seam down the center. Place in the prepared pans, seam side up. Generously brush the tops with canola oil. Cover loosely with plastic wrap, allowing for expansion, and refrigerate until the dough rises above the rims of the pans, at least 2 hours or up to 24 hours.

6. Remove the loaves from the refrigerator, uncover, and let stand at room temperature for 1½ hours. About 20 minutes before baking, preheat an oven to 375°F and position a rack in the center of the oven.

7. Brush the tops of the loaves with the honey mixture. Bake for 55 to 65 minutes, or until the tops are light brown and the loaves sound hollow when tapped with your finger. Cover loosely with aluminum foil halfway through baking if the loaves brown too much. Remove from the pans to cool on a rack.

Bread-Machine Sesame-Honey Oatmeal Bread

1½-pound loaf

1¼ cups water

3 tablespoons butter, melted

¼ cup honey

3 cups bread flour

½ cup rolled oats

1½ tablespoons sesame seeds

3 teaspoons vital wheat gluten

1 teaspoon salt

2 teaspoons bread machine yeast

Rolled oats, for sprinkling

1-pound loaf

¾ cup water

2 tablespoons butter, melted

3 tablespoons honey

2 cups bread flour

⅓ cup rolled oats

1 tablespoon sesame seeds

2 teaspoons vital wheat gluten

½ teaspoon salt

1½ teaspoons bread machine yeast

Rolled oats, for sprinkling

1. Place all of the ingredients, except the oats for sprinkling, in the pan according to the manufacturer's instructions. Set crust on medium and program for the basic bread or delayed time bake cycle; press Start. After the rise, carefully lift the lid and sprinkle with the rolled oats. Close the lid and continue the cycle.

2. After the baking cycle ends, remove the bread from the pan and place on a rack to cool to room temperature.

These dinner rolls are streaked with sun-dried tomatoes and infused with the flavor of fresh herbs. Serve with a soft wedge of room-temperature Teleme cheese or slices of Vermont cheddar, accompanied by a glass of chilled white wine.

Oaten Rolls with Herbs and Sun-Dried Tomatoes

Makes 20 rolls

Sponge

1 tablespoon (1 package) active dry yeast

1 tablespoon light brown sugar

2 cups warm water (105° to 115°F)

½ cup whole-wheat flour

½ cup bread flour

1¼ cups rolled oats

Dough

¼ cup good-quality olive oil

2 teaspoons salt

4 to 4½ cups bread flour

2 tablespoons minced fresh basil, dill, or rosemary

1 cup well-drained oil-packed sun-dried tomatoes, coarsely chopped

Sun-dried tomato oil, for brushing

1. **To make the sponge:** In a large bowl, combine the yeast, sugar, and water. Add the whole-wheat and bread flours and oats; beat hard with a large whisk until creamy. Cover with plastic wrap and set aside at room temperature until bubbly and double in bulk, about 1 hour.

2. **To make the dough:** In a large bowl using a whisk or in the bowl of a heavy-duty electric mixer fitted with the paddle attachment, combine the sponge, olive oil, salt, and 1 cup of the bread flour. Beat hard for 1 minute. Add the herbs and tomatoes. Add the remaining bread flour, ½ cup at a time, mixing on low speed until a soft, shaggy dough that just clears the sides of the bowl forms, switching to a wooden spoon when necessary if making by hand.

3. Turn the dough out onto a lightly floured work surface and gently knead until the dough is soft, smooth, and springy, 1 to 2 minutes for a machine-mixed dough and 3 to 5 minutes for a hand-mixed dough, dusting with flour only 1 tablespoon at a time, just enough as needed to prevent sticking. Place in a lightly greased deep container, turn once to coat the top, and cover with plastic wrap. Let rise at room temperature until double in bulk, 1½ to 2 hours.

4. Grease 20 standard muffin cups (you will need 2 muffin tins). Turn the dough out onto the work surface and divide into 4 equal portions. Divide each portion into 5 equal pieces. Form each piece into a tight 2-inch ball and place in a prepared muffin cup, seam side down. Using floured kitchen shears, snip an X about 1 inch deep in the top of each roll. Brush with the tomato oil. Cover loosely with plastic wrap and let rise until double in bulk, about 45 minutes.

5. About 20 minutes before baking, preheat an oven to 375°F and position a rack in the center of the oven.

6. Bake the rolls until browned, 20 to 25 minutes. Remove from the pans and serve hot, or cool on a rack and reheat before serving.

Fluffy and hearty, these are among the most beloved loaves of oatmeal bread. The recipe comes from my friend Connie Rothermel, whose mother made large batches, enough to share with neighbors or to sell. The variation with almonds and walnuts is also delicious.

Minnesota Oatmeal Egg Bread

Makes two 9-by-5-inch loaves

1½ cups boiling water

1 cup rolled oats

½ cup light molasses

6 tablespoons (¾ stick) unsalted butter or margarine

2 tablespoons (2 packages) active dry yeast

5 to 5½ cups bread flour

1 tablespoon salt

2 large eggs

1. In a large bowl using a wooden spoon or in the bowl of a heavy-duty electric mixer fitted with the paddle attachment, combine the boiling water, rolled oats, molasses, and butter. Stir to melt the butter and let stand until warm, about 30 minutes.

2. Sprinkle the yeast over the oat mixture and let stand 5 minutes to dissolve. Add 1 cup of the bread flour, the salt, and the eggs; beat for 2 minutes, or until very smooth. Add the remaining bread flour, ½ cup at a time, mixing on low speed until a soft, shaggy dough that just clears the sides of the bowl forms, switching to a wooden spoon when necessary if making by hand.

3. Turn the dough out onto a lightly floured work surface and knead until very soft and springy, 1 to 2 minutes for a machine-mixed dough and 3 to 5 minutes for a hand-mixed dough, dusting with flour only 1 tablespoon at a time, just enough as needed to prevent sticking. Do not add too much flour or the dough will stiffen up. Place in a lightly greased deep container, turn once to coat the top, and cover with plastic wrap. Let rise at room temperature until double in bulk, 1½ to 2 hours.

4. Generously grease the bottom and sides two 9-by-5-inch loaf pans. Turn the dough out onto the work surface and divide into 2 equal portions. Pat each into a rectangle and role into a loaf shape. Place in the prepared pans, seam side down. Cover loosely with plastic wrap and let rise until the dough is about 1 inch above the rims of the pans, about 1 hour.

5. About 20 minutes before baking, preheat an oven to 375°F and position a rack in the center of the oven.

6. Using a sharp knife, make 3 diagonal slashes no more than ¼ inch deep down the top center of each loaf. Bake for 40 to 45 minutes, or until the tops are light brown, the sides slightly contract from the pans, and the loaves sound hollow when tapped with your finger. Remove from the pans to cool on racks.

Minnesota Oatmeal Egg Bread with Almonds and Walnuts:

Add ½ cup toasted slivered almonds and ½ cup chopped walnuts to the batter with the eggs in Step 2. Continue to mix, rise, and bake as directed.

There are many variations on soda bread, all quite delicious. This basic plain loaf, via my relatives who hail from County Cork, is rich and chewy from the combination of whole grains. I like warm slices spread with butter and Rose's Lime Marmalade imported from England. You can sweeten this bread with a cup of golden raisins, but I like the bread plain.

Irish Oatmeal Soda Bread

Makes 2 small round loaves

1¾ cups unbleached all-purpose flour

1 cup whole-wheat or whole-grain spelt flour

1 cup quick-cooking Irish oats

3 tablespoons packed light brown sugar

2 teaspoons baking soda

1 teaspoon cream of tartar

1 teaspoon salt

About 1 cup buttermilk

5 tablespoons unsalted butter, melted

1 large egg

1. Preheat an oven to 425°F and position a rack in the center of the oven. Grease a baking sheet or line with parchment paper.

2. In a large bowl, combine the all-purpose and whole-wheat or spelt flours, oats, brown sugar, baking soda, cream of tartar, and salt. In another bowl, combine buttermilk, butter, and egg with a whisk. Make a well in the center of the dry ingredients, add the buttermilk mixture, and stir with a wooden spoon just to moisten. Turn out onto a lightly floured surface and knead gently until dough just comes together, about 5 times. It will feel like a soft biscuit dough. Divide the dough into 2 equal portions and shape each into a round. Place on the prepared baking sheet.

3. Using a sharp knife, make an X about ½ inch deep in the top of each loaf. Bake for 10 minutes, then reduce the oven temperature to 375°F and bake for 30 to 35 minutes longer, or until brown and crusty. Serve warm or let cool on the baking sheet and serve at room temperature.

I like bran muffins to be hearty yet tender, with a strong grain flavor and a subtle sweetness. Unadorned, these high-domed beauties are my idea of a perfect morning muffin.

Oat Bran Morning Muffins

Makes 12 muffins

2½ cups oat bran

2 cups buttermilk

⅓ cup canola oil

½ cup packed light brown sugar

¾ cup dried cranberries or currants

1 large apple or firm pear, peeled, cored, and coarsely chopped

2 large eggs

1½ cups white whole-wheat flour

1½ teaspoons baking powder

1 teaspoon baking soda

2 teaspoons ground cinnamon

½ teaspoon freshly ground nutmeg

½ teaspoon salt

1. Preheat an oven to 375°F and position a rack in the center of the oven. Grease 12 standard muffin cups.

2. In a large bowl, combine the oat bran, buttermilk, oil, and brown sugar. Stir with a whisk until evenly moistened. Add the dried cranberries and apple. Let stand at room temperature for 20 minutes. Add the eggs and whisk to combine.

3. In another bowl, combine the whole-wheat flour, baking powder, baking soda, cinnamon, nutmeg, and salt. Add to the buttermilk mixture and stir briskly with a large spatula or spoon just until evenly moistened, using no more than 15 to 20 strokes. Spoon the batter into the prepared muffin cups until just level with the tops.

4. Bake for 20 to 25 minutes, or until the tops are brown and feel dry and springy, and a cake tester inserted into the center comes out clean. Let the muffins rest in the pan for 5 minutes before removing to a rack to cool.

Quinoa

Quinoa (pronounced *keen-wah*) is not a true grain, but the dried fruit of the goosefoot family, brightly colored herb plants related to spinach and lamb's-quarter. In a family of hundreds of weeds, the few types cultivated for food are known as grain cheno-pods. This edible seed is usually compared with amaranth, as it was a staple, or "mother grain," to the Incas of South America. Quinoa is a frost-resistant plant that tolerates lack of rain and poor soil. It is per-fect for growing above 10,000 feet, although it grows just as well at sea level, on cold, rugged plateaus and terraced valleys. Quinoa also shows up as a preferred crop in the Himachal Pradesh region of the Himalaya in Asia.

Quinoa translates to "mother" in Quechua, a main language of the Andean peoples and Incan descendants. A staple highland grain of equal impor-tance as maize, it was considered the source of strength and endurance for working in the thin mountain air. Quinoa was of such sacred religious and cultural importance to the Incans that the Spanish conquista-dors under Francisco Pizarro restricted cultivation to crops for feeding the poor. Ironically, it is Pizarro who is credited with naming the grain. According to Incan lore, he climbed to view a quinoa field and exclaimed *"Quimera"* ("Wild") at the sight of the brilliant pink, red, and yellow-gold seed heads and tall stalks with edible leaves. Growing the (mispronounced) grain was eventually abandoned by the Incas, but other farmers continued to grow the stigmatized grain in the remote *altiplano* areas of Ecuador, Peru, Argentina, and Bolivia as an ingredient for tortilla flatbreads.

Quinoa was virtually lost to the world until the 1880s, when it was brought to the United States by visionary horticulturalist Luther Burbank. The "for-gotten cereal of the ancients," as he dubbed it, did not catch on. It resurfaced in 1982 in test plots in the high altitudes of the cool, semiarid San Luis Valley in the Rocky Mountains of Colorado, through the efforts of Steven Gorad and Don McKinley. They founded the Quinoa Corporation, the largest seller of Bolivian quinoa, packaged under the name Ancient Harvest Quinoa. Cusack had driven around the San Luis Valley of Colorado to find a farmer willing to let him plant a five-acre test plot. Ernie New, a potato farmer living at the foot of the Sangre de Christo Mountains, let Cusack plant the quinoa, which flourished during a drought year with only one watering. New then tested at least three hundred strains to find good commercial prospects, and today is the mail-order source for domestic organic quinoa and quinoa flour.

Quinoa is the most famous of the so-called super-grains, touted as foods that contribute to overall health today. Like millet, it has plenty of amino acids, more than any of the true grains. The National Academy of Sciences lists quinoa as the highest source of protein in the vegetable kingdom. Quinoa is also high in linoleic acid, starch, sugar, fiber, vitamins, and minerals. It is a complement to both grains and beans, making a com-plete protein, a boon to vegetarian diets. Quinoa is a good food for those unable to eat wheat. It is very light and extremely digestible.

The round, flat quinoa disk is a cross between a sesame seed and a grain of millet. When cooked, the grain turns translucent and fluffy and has a mild flavor with a gentle tangy aftertaste, along with a slightly crunchy texture. A hooplike bran layer surrounds each grain; after cooking, it resembles a half moon or curly tail. An opaque dot in the center disappears when the grain is completely cooked. If left to rest covered after cooking, the grains will swell a bit more.

The highest grade of imported quinoa, *altiplano*, comes from the highest altitudes and has a pale ivory color. The next grade, valley variety, is also mountain grown, usually in Colombia and Peru; it is creamy to pale yellow. The third grade, tan in color, is grown at sea level in Chile. Imported quinoa is rinsed and dried before packaging to kill the germ so the grain will not sprout. Imported quinoa grains are slightly larger than domestic and cook up to a greater volume. Domestic quinoa has a slightly stronger flavor and is flecked with some black seeds. Quinoa grains are coated with a natural resiny compound, saponin, which is bitter and soapy in flavor. The grain needs to be thoroughly rinsed before cooking to dissolve the compound.

Adding the warm cooked grain to yeast and cornmeal batters helps baked goods retain moisture and lightness. Quinoa is great in combination with high-protein wheat flour. At most, use a one-to-five ratio of quinoa flour to wheat flour, or one cup quinoa flour to five cups wheat flour. Quinoa also complements whole-grain amaranth and teff.

Types of Products

Whole raw quinoa is the whole grain rinsed to remove the saponin.

Whole-grain black quinoa, a mix of taupe, chocolate, and russet grains, is stronger in flavor than beige quinoa.

Quinoa flour is the finely ground whole grain. Quinoa flour is sometimes difficult to find, so it is a great grain for home milling. It can be ground into a coarse flour in a food processor fitted with the steel blade. If using a processor, add 3 tablespoons of the flour you will be mixing it with, to aid in grinding.

French bread is the basis for all European peasant breads made with wheat flour. The addition of whole wheat and quinoa in this recipe is certainly an untraditional variation, but results in a delicious bread with a surprisingly moist, tender crumb.

Quinoa Whole-Wheat French Bread

Makes 3 baguettes

2 cups whole-wheat flour

1 cup whole raw quinoa

2 cups warm water (105° to 115°F)

2 teaspoons (¾ package) active dry yeast

1 to 1½ cups bread flour

2 tablespoons vital wheat gluten

2 teaspoons salt

2 tablespoons olive oil

Coarse semolina or farina, for sprinkling

1. Combine 1 cup of the whole-wheat flour and the quinoa in a food processor fitted with the metal blade. Process until a coarse flour forms; set aside.

2. In a large bowl using a whisk or in the bowl of a heavy-duty electric mixer fitted with the paddle attachment, combine the water and yeast. Stir to dissolve and let stand for 5 minutes. Add the whole-wheat–quinoa flour and the remaining 1 cup whole-wheat flour, and beat hard for 2 minutes, switching to a wooden spoon when necessary if making by hand. Add ½ cup of the bread flour and the gluten, salt, and oil and beat for 2 minutes longer. Add the remaining bread flour, ¼ cup at a time, beating on low speed until a soft dough that is hard to mix and pulls up in moist strands forms, using a wooden spoon if making by hand. Cover and let rest for 10 minutes. Continue to add small amounts of bread flour just until the dough clears the sides of the bowl.

3. Turn the dough out onto a lightly floured work surface and knead until the dough just holds its shape, but is quite soft and sticky, 1 to 3 minutes for a machine-mixed dough and 3 to 5 minutes for a hand-mixed dough, dusting with flour only ½ tablespoon at a time,

continued

just enough as needed to prevent sticking. Do not add too much flour, or the dough will be hard and the bread will be dry. Place in a lightly greased deep container, turn once to coat the top, and cover with two layers of plastic wrap. Let rise in the refrigerator for at least 8 hours or up to 12 hours, or overnight.

4. Grease a baking sheet or line with parchment paper and sprinkle with semolina. Turn the dough out onto the work surface and divide into 3 equal portions. Pat each portion into a rectangle and roll tightly into a long sausage shape; roll back and forth with your palms to adjust the length to about 15 inches. Place the baguettes 4 inches apart on the prepared sheet. Cover loosely with plastic wrap and let rise until puffy, about 1½ hours.

5. About 20 minutes before baking, preheat an oven to 425°F and position a rack in the center of the oven.

6. Dust the tops with flour. Using a sharp knife, make 3 diagonal slashes no more than ¼ inch deep across the top of each loaf. Bake for 25 to 30 minutes, or until the baguettes are brown and sound hollow when tapped with your finger. Remove from the sheet to cool on a rack.

Bread-Machine Quinoa Whole-Wheat French Bread

1½-pound loaf

1½ cups whole-wheat flour

⅓ cup whole raw quinoa

1¼ cups water

1½ tablespoons olive oil

1¼ cups bread flour

3 teaspoons vital wheat gluten

1 teaspoon salt

2 teaspoons bread machine yeast

1-pound loaf

1 cup whole-wheat flour

¼ cup whole raw quinoa

¾ cup water

1 tablespoon olive oil

¾ cup bread flour

2 teaspoons vital wheat gluten

½ teaspoon salt

1¼ teaspoons bread machine yeast

1. Combine 1 cup of the whole-wheat flour and the quinoa in a food processor fitted with the metal blade. Process until a coarse flour forms.

2. Place all of the ingredients in the pan according to the manufacturer's instructions. Set crust on medium and program for French bread cycle; press Start.

3. After the baking cycle ends, remove the bread from the pan and place on a rack to cool.

This unique tortilla recipe is adapted from a recipe in a little-known South American cookbook, Comidas Del Ecuador *by Michelle O. Fried. More complicated than the basic flour and corn varieties, these tortillas have vegetables, cheese, herbs, and oats, as well as quinoa. A must for serious tortilla lovers, they make great quesadillas and chilequilles.*

Quinoa Tortillas

Makes sixteen 6-inch tortillas

½ cup whole raw quinoa

1 cup water

2 small shallots, minced

½ cup grated carrot

½ cup minced red bell pepper

1 large egg or ¼ cup liquid egg substitute

¾ cup old-fashioned or quick-cooking oats

¾ cup whole-wheat pastry flour

¾ cup unbleached all-purpose flour

⅓ cup grated Parmesan cheese

½ teaspoon salt

½ teaspoon crumbled dried oregano

1. Place the quinoa in a deep bowl and add cold water to cover. Swirl with your fingers, drain in a fine-mesh sieve, and rinse under cold running water. Repeat until foam no longer rises to the surface when the quinoa is swished in water.

2. In a small saucepan over high heat, bring the water to a rolling boil. Add the quinoa, reduce the heat to the lowest setting, cover, and cook until the water is absorbed and the quinoa is tender, about 20 minutes. Remove from heat and let stand for 15 to 30 minutes uncovered. Use the quinoa while still warm.

3. In a bowl using a wooden spoon or in the bowl of a heavy-duty electric mixer fitted with the paddle attachment, combine the shallots, carrot, bell pepper, and egg, beating on the lowest speed. Add the warm quinoa, oats, whole-wheat and all-purpose flours, cheese, salt, and oregano, mixing just until the dough holds together in a very soft ball and clears the sides of the bowl. Adjust the consistency by adding 1 or 2 table-spoons of flour or 1 egg, if necessary. Turn the dough out onto a lightly floured work surface and briefly knead until it forms a smooth ball, no more than 10 turns. Pat into a cylinder, wrap in plastic wrap to

continued

prevent drying, and let rest at room temperature for 15 minutes.

4. To shape the tortillas, divide the dough into 16 equal portions about the size of a golf ball. Place each portion between 2 pieces of plastic wrap or waxed paper coated with nonstick cooking spray. Press in a tortilla press, turning at regular intervals, until the desired thickness, or roll out with a thin rolling pin to a 6-inch round less than ¼ inch thick. Often the edges will crack; you can leave them, or press on the plastic to smooth or trim with a knife. Leave in the plastic wrap until ready to cook. The pile of tortillas may be refrigerated for up to 8 hours before baking.

5. To bake the tortillas, heat an ungreased heavy cast-iron skillet, griddle, or comal over medium-high heat until drops of water sprinkled on the surface dance across it. Peel off both layers of the plastic and place each tortilla onto the hot pan, one at a time or as many that will fit without touching. Cook for 30 seconds on the first side, turn, and cook for 1 minute. Turn back to the first side and cook for a final 30 seconds. The tortilla will puff up and be speckled with brown spots. The tortillas can be baked in advance, stacked, wrapped in plastic or placed in a thick plastic bag, and refrigerated overnight. Rewarm as needed right before serving.

This drier, baked version of the tamale is a favorite regional recipe throughout the Southwest. Creamed corn gives the bread moistness, green chiles provide a bit of spice, and two cheeses serve as a creamy counterpoint. The bread needs no butter and is great with meat and poultry salads.

Quinoa Double-Corn Bread

Makes one 9-inch round

½ cup unbleached all-purpose flour

½ cup quinoa flour

1 cup yellow cornmeal, fine or medium grind

2 tablespoons sugar

2 teaspoons baking powder

½ teaspoon baking soda

½ teaspoon salt

½ cup buttermilk

1½ cups canned creamed corn

3 large eggs

¼ cup corn oil

One 4-ounce can green chiles, drained and chopped, or ½ cup chopped roasted Anaheim chiles

½ cup (2 ounces) Monterey pepper jack, shredded

½ cup (2 ounces) Cheddar cheese, shredded

1. Preheat an oven to 375°F and position a rack in the center of the oven. Generously grease a 9-inch springform pan, pie plate, or preheated cast-iron skillet.

2. In a large bowl, combine the all-purpose and quinoa flours, cornmeal, sugar, baking powder, baking soda, and salt. In another bowl using a whisk or an electric mixer, combine the buttermilk, creamed corn, eggs, oil, and chiles. Add to the dry ingredients, stirring with a spoon or spatula just until blended. Do not overmix. Gently fold in the cheeses to distribute evenly. Pour into the prepared pan.

3. Bake for 30 to 35 minutes, or until golden around the edges and a cake tester inserted into the center comes out clean. Let stand in the pan for 15 minutes before cutting into wedges to serve.

Mandarin oranges, small citrus fruits with a pleasing sweetness, are a favorite addition to Mexican baked goods. In these refreshing muffins, the tiny segments become sweet pockets that burst in your mouth. I use canned Mandarins packed in their own juice, but the syrup-packed segments are also fine. Orange juice and zest give the muffins a particularly intense orange flavor.

Orange Quinoa Muffins

Makes 12 muffins

1½ cups unbleached all-purpose flour

½ cup quinoa flour

1 teaspoon baking powder

½ teaspoon baking soda

½ teaspoon salt

½ cup (1 stick) unsalted butter, at room temperature

1 cup granulated sugar

2 large eggs

Grated zest of 2 oranges

¾ cup sour cream

½ cup fresh orange juice

One 11-ounce can Mandarin orange segments, drained

About 18 white or Demerara brown sugar cubes, coarsely crushed

1. Preheat an oven to 350°F and position a rack in the center of the oven. Grease 12 standard muffin cups.

2. In a bowl, combine the all-purpose and quinoa flours, baking powder, baking soda, and salt. In another bowl, cream the butter and sugar until fluffy. Add the eggs and zest, beating until well blended. Add the flour mixture to the butter mixture alternately with the sour cream and orange juice, beating well after each addition to make a thick, creamy batter. Gently fold in the orange segments with a large spatula to distribute them evenly, taking care not to break up the segments. Spoon into the prepared muffin cups until three-fourths full. Sprinkle with the crushed sugar.

3. Bake for 20 to 25 minutes, or until the tops are golden, dry, and springy to the touch, and a cake tester inserted into the center comes out clean. Let cool in the pan for 5 minutes before removing to a rack. Serve warm.

Rice

Labeled the "tyrant with a soul" by writer Margaret Visser, rice takes as much back-breaking energy to grow as its precious grains give back in satisfying food nutrition. The amount of organization needed to develop rice-growing technology has given rise to the theory that civilization developed from having to coordinate communal efforts to grow the grain—no small matter when harnessing water in canals, artificial irrigation ditches, terraces, reservoirs, and dikes. In many cultures, rice is, indeed, the staff of life. The words for meal and food in China and Japan translate as rice. The Arabs call rice *aish*, "life," also their name for wheat. It is paired with barley in the Koran, the two grains touted as the "twin sons of heaven."

There are two types of rice. *Indica* refers to long-grained rice like basmati from India; *japonica*, to sticky short grains from China and Japan. Rice grows on a slender grasslike stalk, two to five feet high, with narrow leaves. It requires about four inches of lukewarm moving water and matures in about four months, after alternating periods of being flooded and draining off. During this time, rice is continually nourished by floating algae and water ferns, which convert nitrogen into instant fertilizer. Some rice grows so quickly while being flooded that it shoots up ten inches per day.

According to Margaret Visser, the first rice gathering was done by a race of Neolithic peoples living in Southeast Asia. Archaeological sites in northern Vietnam place the deed five to ten thousand years before Christ, certainly earlier than the cereal cultures of the Middle East. Sealed jars unearthed in China and dating back seven thousand years were found to contain rice.

In China, rice was grown in paddies according to the design of Emperor Shen Nung in 2800 B.C., and the success of this crop around the Yangtze delta was so phenomenal that it was for a long time a guarded secret. The demand for the grain spread quickly throughout all of Buddhist Asia and Japan. The sea-going Persians brought rice back from their spice-gathering India journeys to the Euphrates Valley. Alexander the Great carried rice back to Greece after his invasion of India in the fourth century B.C. Centuries later, the Viscount of Milan introduced the first rice to the Po River valley of Italy, one of the most famous rice producing lands today.

The Arabs and Turks carried rice across southern Europe and northern Africa, even though the African continent has indigenous species of rice. The Moors planted rice on the island of Madagascar, said to have some of the finest rice in the world, and carried it with them as they advanced into Europe. The Portuguese and Spanish, in turn, took rice to their tropical South America colonies.

Seed came to South Carolina from Madagascar when a small bagful was given by a sea captain to Dr. Henry Woodward for his home garden in 1671. Rice cultivation was fully developed in the tidewater marshes, using slave labor, by the time of the American Revolution. Thomas Jefferson, an avid agriculturalist, collected seed from his world travels to find the best strains. After the devastation of the Civil War, rice cultivation was moved to the Mississippi Delta and then to south Texas and California.

Thousands of rice varieties are grown around the world today, each with its own distinct flavor, texture, aroma, color, and degree of translucency. The type of rice you use in breads dictates the final flavor of the loaf. White rice adds just moisture and texture, while aromatic brown and black rices add earthy flavor.

Mild-tasting rice tempers more assertive grains like rye, millet, and buckwheat.

Brown rice has lots of complex carbohydrates, almost a full panel of protein, and almost no fat. It is full of B vitamins and a source of insoluble fiber, iron, calcium, and potassium. When the bran is removed to make white rice, the grains are enriched with thiamine (vitamin B1). Brown rice is nutritionally superior to white rice; enrichment does not replace fiber. Since rice needs treatment with pesticides and fungicides, many bakers seek out organic brands.

Rice flour absorbs moisture more slowly than wheat flours and has a light, sweet flavor. White rice flour is delicate and richer in starch than wheat flour. Brown rice flour includes the bran and germ, and is a bit more tan in color, but is still finely milled. It makes for a slightly denser baked product than white rice flour, but is great in breads. The crust will be a delicate light brown, and the crumb fine. I use the two flours interchangeably.

Rice flour has no gluten, so only a small amount can be added to yeast doughs. Use one to two cups cooked rice to six cups wheat flour for the best results in yeast breads. Use a small proportion—a one-to-five ratio—of rice flour to wheat flour, or a scant one cup rice flour to five cups wheat flour.

Types of Products

White rice is the hulled whole grain that is polished to remove the germ and bran. Short-grain rice, such as Italian arborio rice and Japanese glutinous rice, has a sweet, sticky starch. Medium-grain rice is twice as long as it is wide and is less glutinous. Long-grain rice is four to five times as long as it is wide; it cooks into separate, fluffy grains.

Brown rice is the hulled whole grain with the germ and bran intact and is therefore higher in fiber and nutrients than white rice. It comes in long and short grain.

Rice bran is the separated, oil-rich, tan outer layer. Use like oat bran. Rice polish, a by-product of polishing, includes the bran and germ.

Rice meal is coarsely ground, like grits. It is a great breakfast porridge. It is very similar in texture to couscous.

Rice flour is finely ground white or brown rice. It is not interchangeable with sweet rice flour, a thickener ground from glutinous rice and used in desserts, noodles, and dim sum doughs.

I make some form of banana bread every week and always have backup loaves available in the freezer for quick slicing or gift giving. I prefer this bread without any embellishments, to savor its moist, smooth texture. The bread is best the day after it is made. Wrapped tightly in plastic wrap, it will keep in the refrigerator for up to four days.

Sour Cream Banana Bread

Makes four 5¾-by-3¼-inch loaves

½ cup vegetable oil

1 cup sugar

2 large eggs

1 teaspoon pure vanilla extract

2 or 3 medium to large overripe bananas, slightly mashed to make 1 cup

½ cup sour cream

1 cup unbleached all-purpose flour

½ cup brown rice flour

1 teaspoon baking soda

½ teaspoon salt

1. Preheat an oven to 350°F and position a rack in the center of the oven. Grease four 5¾-by-3¼-inch loaf pans and dust with flour.

2. In a bowl, combine the oil, sugar, and eggs. Beat hard with a whisk or electric mixer until light colored and creamy, about 1 minute. Add the vanilla and beat again until well combined. Add the mashed bananas and sour cream, and beat until smooth. Combine the all-purpose and brown rice flours, baking soda, and salt. Add to the banana-egg mixture and beat well until evenly combined and creamy. Divide among the prepared pans and place the pans on a baking sheet.

3. Bake for 35 to 40 minutes, or until the tops are firm to the touch, the sides slightly contract from the pan, and a cake tester inserted into the center comes out clean. Remove from the pans to cool on a rack.

This moist bread is comfort food. It is the perfect loaf for sandwiches and toast.

Harvest Bread

Makes two 9-by-5-inch loaves

1 cup water

½ cup short-grain brown rice

5 to 5½ cups bread flour

1 cup brown rice flour

½ cup whole-wheat flour, plus 4 teaspoons for dusting

½ cup dry buttermilk powder

1½ tablespoons (1½ packages) active dry yeast

1 tablespoon salt

2 cups hot water (120°F)

⅓ cup unsalted butter, melted, or ⅓ cup vegetable or nut oil

⅓ cup honey, warmed

2 large eggs

1. In a small saucepan, bring the water to a boil. Add the rice and bring back to a boil. Cover and reduce heat to a simmer. Cook 45 minutes. Cool or chill. Measure out ¾ cup cooked rice, reserving the remaining rice for another use.

2. In a large bowl using a whisk or in the bowl of a heavy-duty electric mixer fitted with the paddle attachment, combine 1 cup of the bread flour and the brown rice flour, ½ cup whole-wheat flour, buttermilk powder, yeast, and salt. Add the hot water. Beat hard until creamy, about 1 minute. Add the melted butter, honey, eggs, and brown rice. Beat for 1 minute longer. Add the remaining bread flour, ½ cup at a time, beating on low speed until a soft dough that just clears the sides of the bowl forms, switching to a wooden spoon when necessary if making by hand. The dough will be slightly stiff and very sticky.

3. Turn the dough out onto a lightly floured work surface and knead until soft and springy, 1 to 2 minutes for a machine-mixed dough and 3 to 5 minutes for a hand-mixed dough, dusting with flour only 1 tablespoon at a time, just enough as needed to prevent sticking. The dough will be moist and slightly tacky. Place the dough in a lightly greased deep container, turn once to coat the top, and cover with plastic wrap.

Let rise at room temperature until double in bulk, about 2 hours. Do not worry or rush the dough if it takes longer.

4. Grease two 9-by-5-inch loaf pans. Turn the dough out onto a clean work surface and divide into 2 equal portions. Pat each portion into a rectangle and roll into a loaf shape. Place the loaves, seam side down, into the prepared pans. Cover loosely with plastic wrap and let rise until the dough is puffy and about 1 inch above the rims of the pans, about 45 minutes.

5. About 20 minutes before baking, preheat an oven to 375°F and position a rack in the center of the oven.

6. Using a sharp knife, make 1 long slash no more than ¼ inch deep down the center of each loaf. Dust the top of each loaf with 2 teaspoons whole-wheat flour. Bake for 35 to 40 minutes, or until the loaves are deep brown, the sides slightly contract from the pan, and the loaves sound hollow when tapped with your finger. Remove from the pans to a rack to cool.

Cornmeal-Millet Harvest Bread:

Substitute ½ cup medium-grind yellow cornmeal for the ½ cup whole-wheat flour. Soak 1¼ cups raw whole millet in ¾ cup boiling water for 15 minutes and drain; substitute for the cooked brown rice. Mix, rise, shape, and bake as for Harvest Bread.

Rye and Wild Rice Harvest Bread:

Substitute ½ cup medium rye flour for the ½ cup whole-wheat flour. Substitute ¾ cup cooked wild rice for the ¾ cup brown rice. Mix, rise, shape, and bake as for Harvest Bread.

This recipe is adapted from a now-famous recipe developed by Bette Hagman in The Gluten-Free Gourmet. *Xanthan gum, a powder, is an important addition to wheat-free yeast breads to help them retain their shape. Serve this focaccia the same day it is baked, cut into squares. It is good warm from the oven as a snack or as a sandwich bread cut into wedges.*

Rice Flour Focaccia with Olive Oil and Herbs

Makes one 11-by-17-inch rectangle or six 6-inch rounds

2 cups warm water (105° to 115°F)

¼ cup (4 packages) active dry yeast

2 tablespoons honey

4 cups brown rice flour

4 cups tapioca flour

1½ cups nonfat dry milk powder

8 teaspoons xanthan gum

2 teaspoons salt

1 cup hot water (120°F)

6 tablespoons olive oil

8 large egg whites, at room temperature

Yellow cornmeal, for sprinkling

½ cup olive oil

1 tablespoon crumbled dried oregano or 2 tablespoons finely chopped fresh oregano, or to taste

1 tablespoon crumbled dried basil or 2 tablespoons finely chopped fresh basil, or to taste

1. Pour the warm water into a bowl. Sprinkle the yeast and drizzle the honey over the water. Stir to dissolve and let stand at room temperature until foamy, about 10 minutes.

2. In a large bowl using a whisk or in the bowl of a heavy-duty electric mixer fitted with the paddle attachment, combine the rice and tapioca flours, milk powder, xanthan gum, and salt. Add the hot water and 6 tablespoons olive oil. Beat for 1 minute. Add the yeast mixture and beat for 2 minutes. Add the egg whites and beat hard for 3 minutes. The dough will be thick and batterlike but hold its own shape. Adjust the texture, if necessary, by adding a few more tablespoons of rice flour.

3. Grease an 11-by-17-inch baking sheet or six 6-inch round cake pans at least 1 inch deep, and sprinkle with cornmeal. Using a spatula, transfer the dough to the sheet or divide among the pans. Using your hand enclosed in a plastic bag, pat the dough to fill the pan(s). Cover loosely with plastic wrap and let rise at room temperature for 20 to 30 minutes.

4. Meanwhile, combine the ½ cup olive oil and herbs in a small bowl. Let sit for 20 minutes. Position a rack in the center of an oven, place a baking stone on the rack, and preheat the oven to 450°F for 20 minutes. If not using a stone, preheat the oven to 400°F.

5. Using your fingertips, gently press indentations about ¼ inch deep in the dough. Drizzle with the herb oil, letting it pool in the dimples. Reduce the oven temperature to 400°F if using a stone. Place the pan directly on the hot stone or on the oven rack and bake for 20 to 25 minutes for small rounds or 35 to 40 minutes for a large rectangle, or until nicely browned. Let cool in the pan.

This bread can be made with any short-grain brown rice or blend, but is particularly good with this aromatic earth-red variety.

Bread-Machine Wehani Rice Bread

1½-pound loaf

1¼ cups water

6 tablespoons wehani rice

3 tablespoons olive oil

3 tablespoons honey

2 cups plus 2 tablespoons bread flour

⅓ cup whole-wheat flour

⅓ cup brown rice flour

¼ cup nonfat dry milk

4 teaspoons vital wheat gluten

1 teaspoon salt

1¾ teaspoons bread machine yeast

1-pound loaf

⅞ cup water

4 tablespoons wehani rice

2 tablespoons olive oil

2 tablespoons honey

1½ cups bread flour

¼ cup whole-wheat flour

¼ cup brown rice flour

3 tablespoons nonfat dry milk

3 teaspoons vital wheat gluten

¾ teaspoon salt

1¼ teaspoons bread machine yeast

1. In a small saucepan, bring the water to a boil. Add the rice and simmer until tender, 25 minutes. Cool and add enough water to make 1¼ cups or ⅞ cup, depending on the loaf size desired.

2. Place all of the ingredients in the pan according to the manufacturer's instructions. Set crust on medium and program for the basic bread cycle; press Start.

3. After the baking cycle ends, remove the bread from the pan, and place on a rack to cool.

This classic buttermilk biscuit recipe has three parts dry ingredients to one part tangy liquid to create a dough that rises high and forms a crisp crust when baked.

Smoked Gouda Biscuits

Makes twelve to fourteen 2-inch dinner biscuits

2 tablespoons brown rice flour, for sprinkling

2 tablespoons cornmeal, for sprinkling

1 cup unbleached all-purpose flour

1 cup brown rice flour

¼ cup chopped fresh chives

2 teaspoons baking powder

½ teaspoon baking soda

½ teaspoon salt

6 tablespoons unsalted butter, margarine, or solid vegetable shortening, cut into pieces

1 cup grated smoked Gouda cheese

1 cup buttermilk

1. Preheat an oven to 400°F and position a rack in the center of the oven. Grease a baking sheet or line with parchment paper and sprinkle with the 2 tablespoons rice flour and 2 tablespoons cornmeal.

2. In a bowl, combine the all-purpose and brown rice flours, chives, baking powder, baking soda, and salt. Cut the butter into the dry ingredients with a pastry blender or 2 knives until the mixture resembles coarse crumbs. If the butter gets very soft, refrigerate the mixture for 20 minutes. Add the cheese and buttermilk, stirring just to moisten all the ingredients. The dough will be slightly shaggy, but not sticky.

3. Turn the dough out onto a lightly floured work surface. Knead gently until the dough just holds together, about 10 times. Pat the dough into a rectangle about 1 inch thick. Do not add too much flour or the biscuits will be tough. Using a 2½-inch biscuit cutter dipped in flour, press down firmly without twisting to make biscuits. Cut as close together as possible for a minimum of leftover dough. Gently press the scraps together and cut out additional biscuits. Place ½ inch apart on the prepared baking sheet.

4. Bake for 15 to 18 minutes, or until golden brown. Serve hot.

Rye

The humble rye plant, *Secale cereale,* looks almost exactly like an extra-tall wheat plant. It is the quintessential European country grain, used in much-beloved, dense, strong-flavored dark loaves. The *Secale* genus is remarkably small. It contains only four species from eastern Europe and the Asia Minor peninsula bordering the Black Sea. *S. anatolicum* and *S. monatumum,* wild varieties, are still found in those areas. The rye weed was almost the last grain to be domesticated, in about the fourth century B.C., and showed up from Turkey to Afghanistan around the first millennium B.C. and later in Greece and Rome. *S. monatumum,* identified as the earliest ancestor of today's rye, was crossed with other wild ryes by Russian biologists, to produce the modern hardy domesticate. It is the nearest relative to wheat of all the cereals.

Domesticated rye became popular in Europe during the Middle Ages and was used to make the basic daily bread. It was brought to Pennsylvania and New York by early Dutch settlers and found a home in the northern Heartland and Canada. This is a grain that is grown by rural peoples in lands with long winters and short growing seasons, and the grains are "parched," or roasted, before storage. Main rye growing states are Texas, Oklahoma, Oregon, and Georgia.

Rye is high in B vitamins, especially niacin. It has plenty of iron, zinc, and magnesium. Rye has vitamin E and rutin, premium antioxidants, as well as insoluble fiber.

Rye has a characteristically bitter-strong, earthy flavor with a pleasant sour aftertaste. Without the addition of wheat flour for body, rye makes a flat, crumbly, and coarse-grained loaf, although many favorite fermented Scandinavian and Russian breads are made in this manner. The more rye flour and the coarser the grind, the stronger the flavor and the slower to rise the bread will be. The flavor of rye is often enhanced by the addition of a small amount of vinegar or caramel.

Rye contains gliaden but not glutenin, so it must be used in combination with high-protein bread flour. Since the gluten proteins in rye are surrounded by a saplike substance (pentosan gum) that is released when water is added to the flour, sourdough is a good leavener for rye breads, as it dissolves the inherent gumminess that obstructs the developing gluten. Favorite rye breads all contain some wheat flour: Jewish rye, pumpernickel, Swedish rye, Russian rye, pretzels. Loaves are usually compact, moist, and good keepers. Rye combines well with the flavors of dill, caraway, anise, fennel, onions, and strong coffee. Rye breads often have cheeses and tangy buttermilk baked into them. Scandinavian rye breads often contain some orange, apples, or applesauce, and dried fruits such as figs, apricots, and raisins naturally complement rye in bread. The French make a famous country bread combining rye, walnuts, and raisins.

For traditional rye breads, use a one-to-one ratio of rye flour to wheat flour, or three cups rye flour to three cups wheat flour. Crusts bake up very dark brown, and the crumb is fine grained. Make certain loaves are well baked; otherwise the bread will be gummy inside. Rye breads are often better the day after they are baked, giving time for the crumb to set.

Types of Products

Whole rye is the whole grain with bran and germ intact.

Rye grits are cracked whole rye. Use like cracked wheat.

Rye meal, or pumpernickel flour, is medium-ground whole rye, which gives a rough texture to breads.

Rye flakes have been steamed and flattened by steel rollers. Use the same way as rolled oats, barley, or wheat.

Rye flour is the finely ground whole grain. The flour varies in color and texture, depending on varying proportions of bran and germ separated by bolting: light, medium, dark. Whole rye flour is usually a medium flour.

White rye flour, a favorite of the professional baking industry, is the ground endosperm of the rye kernel. It does not contain germ or bran and makes the lightest rye bread.

These dense and moist loaves are best when allowed to cool completely. Serve slices with a savory main course or use them to make open-faced sandwiches with melted goat cheese and mozzarella, or smoked salmon and sliced red onion.

Sour Cream Rye

Makes 4 round loaves

Sponge

2 cups tepid water (about 100°F)

1½ tablespoons (2 scant packages) active dry yeast

1 cup nonfat dry milk powder

1 cup sour cream

3 cups rye flour

½ cup rye meal (pumpernickel flour)

¼ cup dark molasses

Dough

4 tablespoons (½ stick) unsalted butter or margarine, melted

4 teaspoons salt

2 tablespoons vital wheat gluten

3 tablespoons caraway seeds

4 to 4½ cups bread flour

1. **To prepare the sponge:** Pour the water into a large bowl or the bowl of a heavy-duty electric mixer. Sprinkle the yeast over the water. Stir with a whisk or the whisk attachment until dissolved. Add the milk powder, sour cream, rye and pumpernickel flours, and molasses. Beat until smooth and thick. Cover loosely with plastic wrap and let stand at room temperature until double in bulk, about 1 hour.

2. **To prepare the dough:** Add the melted butter, salt, gluten, caraway seeds, and 1 cup of the bread flour to the sponge. Beat hard with a wooden spoon for 2 minutes on medium speed with the paddle attachment. Add the remaining bread flour, ½ cup at a time, mixing on low speed until a sticky dough that just clears the sides of the bowl forms, switching to a wooden spoon when necessary if making by hand.

3. Turn the dough out onto a lightly floured surface and knead vigorously until the dough is smooth and very elastic yet still moist and tacky, 1 to 2 minutes for a machine-mixed dough and 3 to 4 minutes for a hand-mixed dough, dusting with flour only 1 tablespoon at a time, just enough as needed to prevent sticking. Place in a lightly greased deep container, turn once to coat the top, and cover with plastic wrap. Let rise at room temperature until double in bulk, 1½ to 2 hours.

4. Grease 2 baking sheets or line with parchment paper. Turn the dough out onto the work surface and divide into 4 equal portions. Knead lightly into rounds. Dust lightly with rye flour and place, smooth side up, on the baking sheets. Let rise, uncovered, until soft and springy, about 1 hour.

5. About 20 minutes before baking, preheat an oven to 350°F and position a rack in the center of the oven.

6. Using a sharp knife, make 4 parallel slashes no more than ¼ inch deep in the top of each loaf. Or make 2 slashes to form an X. Bake 50 to 55 minutes, or until golden brown and crusty. Remove from the sheets to cool on a rack.

This quick version of pumpernickel is a dense, coarse-textured, mildly sweet loaf. Serve plain or toasted, with coffee, fruit salads, or soft spreadable cheeses.

Fig-Pumpernickel Quick Bread

Makes three 5¾-by-3¼-inch loaves

1 cup unbleached all-purpose flour

1 cup medium or dark rye flour

½ cup whole-wheat pastry flour

2 tablespoons wheat bran

¼ cup packed light brown sugar

2 teaspoons baking powder

1 teaspoon baking soda

1½ teaspoons instant espresso powder

1½ teaspoons unsweetened cocoa or carob powder

½ teaspoon salt

8 ounces dried black Mission figs, stemmed and chopped

¼ cup currants

1 cup buttermilk

⅓ cup sour cream

2 tablespoons unsalted butter or margarine, melted

1 large egg

¼ cup dark unsulphured molasses

1. Preheat an oven to 350°F and position a rack in the center of the oven. Grease three 5¾-by-3½-inch loaf pans and dust with flour.

2. In a large bowl, combine the all-purpose, rye, and whole-wheat flours, bran, brown sugar, baking powder, baking soda, espresso, cocoa, and salt. Add the figs and currants and toss until evenly distributed. In a small bowl, combine the buttermilk, sour cream, butter, egg, and molasses. Beat with a whisk until frothy. Make a well in the dry ingredients and pour in the buttermilk mixture. Stir with a large spatula until just evenly moistened. The batter will be very thick. Divide among the prepared pans.

3. Bake for 35 to 40 minutes, or until the tops are crusty and a cake tester inserted into the center comes out clean. Remove from the pans to cool on a rack.

The combination of the rye and wheat flours makes for a soft, high-rising loaf. This is a sweet rye bread in the Scandinavian tradition, with the traditional flavoring of molasses, orange, and seeds.

Bread-Machine Swedish Rye Bread

1½-pound loaf

⅞ cup water

¼ cup orange juice

3 tablespoons molasses

2 tablespoons vegetable oil

1¾ cups bread flour

1 cup medium rye flour

2 tablespoons yellow cornmeal

4 teaspoons vital wheat gluten

2 teaspoons caraway seeds

1 teaspoon fennel seeds

1 teaspoon grated orange zest

1 teaspoon salt

2 teaspoons bread machine yeast

1-pound loaf

½ cup water

3 tablespoons orange juice

2 tablespoons molasses

1 tablespoon vegetable oil

1¼ cups bread flour

⅔ cup medium rye flour

1½ tablespoons yellow cornmeal

3 teaspoons vital wheat gluten

1½ teaspoons caraway seeds

½ teaspoon fennel seeds

½ teaspoon grated orange zest

¾ teaspoon salt

1¼ teaspoons bread machine yeast

1. Place all of the ingredients in the pan according to the manufacturer's instructions. Set crust on medium and program for the basic bread cycle; press Start.

2. After the baking cycle ends, remove the bread from the pan and place on a rack to cool.

Steamed breads are country food. The steaming process results in an exceptionally moist, almost spongy-textured bread. Made with rye, corn, and whole wheat, this bread has one of the great grain flavor combinations. Serve it warm, sliced into rounds. Store wrapped in plastic wrap at room temperature for up to 3 days.

Steamed Rye and Maple Brown Bread

Makes two 1-pound loaves

1 cup golden raisins

3 tablespoons golden rum

1 cup yellow or white cornmeal, preferably stone-ground

1 cup whole-wheat or graham flour

1 cup medium rye flour

½ cup unbleached all-purpose flour

2 teaspoons baking soda

1 teaspoon salt

2 cups buttermilk

¾ cup pure maple syrup

2 large eggs

1. In a small bowl, combine the raisins and the rum. Let stand at room temperature for 1 hour. Generously grease two 1-pound coffee cans, honey cans, or two 4- or 5-cup lidded pudding molds and line the bottoms of the cans with parchment paper.

2. In a large bowl, combine the cornmeal, whole-wheat, rye, and all-purpose flours, baking soda, and salt. In a 4-cup liquid measuring cup, combine the buttermilk, maple syrup, and eggs. Stir with a whisk until combined. Pour into the dry ingredients and add the raisins and rum. Stir well until evenly moistened.

3. Fill each prepared can or mold no more than two-thirds full. Cover tightly with a lid or with aluminum foil held with thick rubber bands. Place on a rack in a deep pot and add boiling water to reach 1 to 2 inches up the sides of the cans or molds. Cover and adjust the heat to maintain a low simmer. Steam for 2 hours, or until a cake tester inserted into the center comes out clean. Add more boiling water during the steaming if too much has evaporated.

4. About 20 minutes before the bread finishes steaming, preheat an oven to 400°F.

5. Uncover the breads and place in the oven for no more than 5 minutes to dry slightly. Remove from the cans or molds, peel off the parchment paper, and cool the loaves on their sides on a rack.

Rye flour is an unusual addition to pan corn bread, but the savory combination results in a hearty breakfast bread.

Rye Corn Bread with Sausage and Apples

Makes one 9-inch cornbread

1 pound uncooked chicken-apple sausage

2 medium tart green cooking apples, peeled, cored, and sliced crosswise into ½-inch rings

¾ cup unbleached all-purpose flour

¾ cup medium rye flour

½ cup fine-grind yellow or white cornmeal, preferably stone-ground

3 tablespoons packed light brown sugar

¼ teaspoon salt

½ teaspoon baking soda

2 large eggs

1 cup buttermilk

⅓ cup corn oil

1. Preheat an oven to 400°F and position a rack in the center of the oven.

2. In a skillet over medium heat, cook the sausage until browned, about 8 minutes. Grease a 9-inch ceramic or glass baking dish with the drippings and extra oil, if needed. Chop the cooked sausage. Sprinkle the bottom of the dish with half of the sausage pieces and lay the apple rings in an overlapping pattern to cover the sausage.

3. In a bowl, combine the all-purpose and rye flours, cornmeal, sugar, salt, and baking soda. In a small bowl, combine the eggs, buttermilk, and oil with a whisk. Add to the dry ingredients with the remaining sausage. Stir until all ingredients are just moistened yet thoroughly blended. Pour over the apples in the pan.

4. Bake for 30 to 35 minutes, or until golden around the edges and a cake tester inserted into the center comes out clean. Let stand 10 minutes before cutting into squares.

Teff

Teff is the least familiar of all the cereal grains and flours to the home baker, having just recently been introduced to the American public through the persistence of a growing number of Ethiopian immigrants who continue to make their beloved staple flatbread from their regional grain.

Teff is by far one of the oldest cereals. It was domesticated before recorded history in the ancient region of Abyssinia, the site of modern-day Ethiopia. One of its botanical names is *Eragrostis abyssinica,* and just rolling the words over my tongue brings visions of the Queen of Sheba of Ethiopian legend, with her pet lion lounging alongside, sitting down to a stewlike meal eaten with her fingers, piled on the circular edible pancake called *injera.* Teff, a member of the millet family known for its excellent storage properties, is still highly preferred in Ethiopia over any other grain and is grown as a major cereal crop, although in some areas it is still collected as a wild grain.

The grain boasts about 2,000 species, all of which are edible, each with different bread-making characteristics. The plants are subtropical, yet have survived because they are drought-resistant; after complete dehydration, a seemingly dead plant will come back to life, the brown parts turning to green, within a few hours after being watered.

The botanical name, *Eragrostis,* comes from the Greek *eros,* meaning "love," and *agrostis,* "grass." The tufted annual known affectionately as "lovegrass" has panicles with miniature many-flowered spikelets that resemble tiny hearts with long drooping branches. The small-grained seeds are the tiniest of any cereal; 150 are needed to equal the size of a grain of wheat.

Teff has been introduced to the United States due to the pioneering efforts of Wayne Carlson, former Peace Corps and Red Cross volunteer to Ethiopia, who developed a taste for the native flatbread. He grows teff in the high desert region of southwest Idaho, a state with loamy volcanic soil not unlike the soil of Ethiopia. Carlson experimented with seven hundred varieties to end up with three cash crops that are marketed to the Ethiopian community, as well as natural-food stores.

Three main types of teff are grown: One is ivory colored with a brown cast (*thaf hagaiz*). Another is mahogany brown. A red variety is available only in specialty markets. The flours retain these colors. The ivory is coveted for making injera. Teff is known for its pleasantly sweet, almost molasseslike flavor, with the brown variety the richest in flavor. Teff is high in protein, and contains seven times more calcium and iron than wheat. It is the best source of soluble fiber next to oats and is packed with minerals, including thiamine, niacin, boron, magnesium, and zinc.

A small proportion of the flour combined with bread flour makes delicious light-textured bread with an earthy color and almost malt-sweet flavor. At most, use a one-to-five ratio of teff flour to wheat flour, or one cup teff flour to five cups wheat flour. To produce home-milled flour, use an electric flour mill; the minute seeds will stick in a food processor.

Types of Products

Whole teff is the whole grain with the bran and germ intact.

Teff flour is the finely ground whole grain. The flour varies in color depending on what type of seed is ground. The most common colors are ivory and brown.

*Pleasantly sweet, yet assertive, teff and mild-flavored
quinoa give this bread a soft, slightly crunchy consistency.*

Teff Honey-Egg Bread

Makes 3 oval loaves

Teff-Quinoa

¼ cup teff

1 cup water

¼ cup whole raw quinoa

Dough

1 cup warm water (105° to 115°F)

1 tablespoon (1 package) active dry yeast

Pinch of sugar or 1 teaspoon honey

1 cup warm milk (105° to 115°F)

½ cup honey

⅓ cup sunflower seed oil

2 large eggs

1 tablespoon salt

1 cup plus 2 tablespoons teff flour

4½ to 5 cups bread flour

1. **To make teff-quinoa:** Place the teff in a skillet over medium heat and toast until light brown. In a small saucepan over high heat, bring the water to a rolling boil. Add the teff and quinoa, reduce the heat to the lowest setting, cover, and cook, stirring twice, until the water is absorbed and the grains are tender, about 10 minutes. Set aside to cool. You should have about 1⅛ cups.

2. **To make the dough:** Pour ½ cup of the warm water into a small bowl. Sprinkle the yeast and sugar over the water. Stir to dissolve, and let stand at room temperature until foamy, about 10 minutes.

3. In a large bowl using a whisk or in the bowl of a heavy-duty electric mixer fitted with the paddle attachment, combine the remaining ½ cup warm water, milk, honey, oil, eggs, and salt. Add the teff-quinoa and beat until smooth. Add the yeast mixture and 1 cup of the teff flour. Beat hard until smooth, about 2 minutes. Add the bread flour, ½ cup at a time, beating on low speed until a soft, shaggy dough that just clears the sides of the bowl forms, switching to a wooden spoon when necessary if making by hand.

4. Turn the dough out onto a lightly floured work surface and knead until smooth and elastic, 1 to 2 minutes for a machine-mixed dough and 3 to 4 minutes for a hand-mixed dough, dusting with flour only 1 tablespoon at a time, just enough as needed to prevent sticking. The dough will be slightly sticky. Place in a lightly greased deep container, turn once to coat the top, and cover with plastic wrap. Let rise at room temperature until double in bulk, 1½ to 2 hours.

5. Grease a baking sheet or line with parchment paper. Turn the dough out onto a lightly floured work surface and divide into 3 equal portions. Form each into an oval loaf. Place on the prepared sheet. Dust the tops with the remaining 2 tablespoons of teff flour. Cover loosely with plastic wrap and let rise until double in bulk, 1 to 1½ hours.

6. About 20 minutes before baking, preheat an oven to 350°F and position a rack in the center of the oven.

7. With a sharp knife, slash one long line down the length of the loaf, no more than ¼ inch deep. Bake for 35 to 40 minutes, or until the loaves are brown and sound hollow when tapped with your finger. Remove from the sheet to cool on a rack.

Bread-Machine Teff Honey-Egg Bread

1½-pound loaf

1 cup water

3 tablespoons oil

¼ cup honey

1 large egg

½ cup cooked teff-quinoa
  (page 104)

2½ cups bread flour

½ cup teff flour

¼ cup nonfat dry milk

5 teaspoons vital wheat gluten

1 teaspoon salt

1¾ teaspoons bread machine
  yeast

1-pound loaf

¾ cup water

2 tablespoons oil

3 tablespoons honey

1 large egg

⅓ cup cooked teff-quinoa
  (page 104)

1⅔ cups bread flour

⅓ cup teff flour

3 tablespoons nonfat dry milk

3 teaspoons vital wheat gluten

¾ teaspoon salt

1¼ teaspoons bread machine
  yeast

1. Place all of the ingredients in the pan according to the manufacturer's instructions. Set crust on medium and program for the basic or whole-wheat bread cycle; press Start.

2. After the baking cycle ends, remove the bread from the pan and place on a rack to cool.

A traditional and very ancient flatbread from Ethiopia, injera is made from a batter leavened with starter kept from a previous batch and sits a few days to ferment. The batter is cooked into crêpelike rounds up to two feet in diameter and used to scoop up food. If you are making the starter from scratch, plan on three days preparation time before baking.

American Injera

Makes about eighteen 9-inch injera

Starter

1 package (½ ounce) commercial dry sourdough starter

2 cups bread flour

2 cups tepid water (85° to 90°F)

Dough

1 cup unbleached all-purpose flour

¾ cup teff flour

½ cup brown rice flour

4½ cups warm water (100°F)

¼ teaspoon baking soda

½ teaspoon salt

1. **To make the starter:** In a bowl, combine the starter and flour. Add the warm water and whisk until smooth. Transfer to a glass jar or crock. Cover loosely with plastic wrap and let stand at room temperature for 48 hours, stirring the mixture 2 to 3 times each day. It will be bubbly and begin to ferment. Measure out 1 cup starter and store the remaining 2 cups in the refrigerator, covered loosely.

2. **To make the dough:** In a large bowl using a whisk or in the bowl of a heavy-duty electric mixer fitted with the whisk attachment, combine the all-purpose, teff, and brown rice flours. Stir or mix on low to aerate. Slowly add the warm water, beating constantly to avoid lumps. Add the starter and mix well until smooth. The batter will be the consistency of that for thin pancakes. Cover and let rest in a warm spot for 24 hours. The dough will bubble and ferment, then naturally deflate.

3. Crush the baking soda with the back of a spoon. Add the baking soda and salt to the dough and mix until smooth.

4. Preheat a round nonstick 9-inch griddle over medium-high heat. Using a ½-cup measure, pour the batter onto the hot griddle, spiraling from the outside to the center and tilting the pan to fill in the empty spots. Cover and cook quickly on one side only until the injera has risen slightly, the top is dry, and the edges curl slightly, 1 to 2 minutes. Do not brown. Using a spatula, transfer to a plate to cool. Cook the remaining injera. If you like, reserve ½ cup of batter and add to the refrigerated starter.

In The Splendid Grain, *author Rebecca Wood writes that teff flour "takes gingerbread to new heights." I took up that challenge and discovered that spicy teff flour adds complexity to this rich, moist version of gingerbread. Serve topped with whipped cream flavored with ground cinnamon.*

Teff Spicebread

Makes one 9-inch square cake

¼ cup chopped crystallized ginger

3 tablespoons finely chopped candied orange peel

3 tablespoons Cognac

1½ cups teff flour

2 cups unbleached all-purpose flour

2 teaspoons baking soda

1 tablespoon ground ginger

1 teaspoon ground cinnamon

½ teaspoon ground cloves

½ teaspoon ground coriander

½ teaspoon freshly ground nutmeg

½ teaspoon dry mustard

¼ teaspoon ground mace

¼ teaspoon ground black pepper

½ teaspoon salt

½ cup (1 stick) unsalted butter, at room temperature

½ cup packed light brown sugar

2 large eggs

1 cup unsulphured molasses

1 cup boiling water

1 tablespoon instant espresso powder

1. Place the crystallized ginger and orange peel in a small bowl. Add the Cognac and let stand for 30 minutes. In a large bowl, combine the teff and all-purpose flours, baking soda, spices, and salt. Set aside.

2. Preheat an oven to 350°F and position a rack in the center of the oven. Coat a 9-inch square pan with nonstick baking spray.

3. In a bowl, cream the butter and brown sugar until fluffy. Add the eggs, one at a time, until incorporated. Add the molasses in a stream, beating constantly. Pour the boiling water into a small bowl. Add the espresso powder and stir until dissolved. Add to the butter mixture, ¼ cup at a time, alternating with the dry ingredients. Stir in the ginger, orange peel, and Cognac. Pour the batter into the prepared pan.

4. Bake for 35 to 40 minutes, or until the top springs back when touched and a cake tester inserted into the center comes out clean. Cool in the pan for 30 minutes. Cut into squares to serve.

Wheat

There are over 30,000 different varieties of wheat, all belonging to fourteen basic species categorized by inherent characteristics and adapted to growing conditions from the Arctic to the tropics. Our common wheat makes up almost all of the wheat grown in the world. The botanical name, *Triticum,* was chosen by Linnaeus from an old Latin name for cereal. The most important of all the cereal grains, wheat is considered a dry fruit. Its structure, typical of the Gramineae family, has one unit that contains both the seed and the fruit of the plant.

Wheat is the best grain for bread making. The outermost bran layers contain the fiber and minerals. The center, a floury mass known as the endosperm, contains starch and gluten. The latter is the substance that gives bread its elastic consistency and supports the action of yeast.

The most important grain crop in the world, it is responsible for the development of the great bread-wheat civilizations from Mesopotamia to India, and China to Egypt, Greece, Rome, and then to our own. Wheat may have originated in the prehistoric Near East, but its cultivation spread quickly. Delving into these origins has fostered an entire branch of science called agricultural archaeology.

If you hang around bread aficionados, two words—*eikorn* and *emmer*—will come up in conversation. Both were grasses that grew wild on the mountain hillsides and fertile plains of the river valleys of Asia Minor. Eikorn, the first ancient original wheat, was discovered 6,700 years ago at Jarmo in eastern Iraq. The kernels were parched and pounded loose from the sticky hulls, then the grains were hand-ground into a mush or thick cake. Emmer, the next stage of wheat evolution, was the grain of choice in ancient Egypt. It was also probably the chief cereal grain in the Near East up into Greco-Roman times. This was the wheat the Egyptians were using when they discovered wild yeasts, which allowed them to give their heavy, ground cakes a new, lighter, fluffier texture.

Emmer wheat is the parent of durum wheat, the large-grained amber wheat used today for pasta and Italian country breads. The Romans grew this wheat and made it the prominent grain of the Mediterranean. A sister of durum is rivet wheat, or "mummy wheat," the wheat that was supposedly brought back from King Tut's tomb to be planted in Montana and which became kamut. Kamut handles like durum wheat and boasts the largest kernels of all cultivated wheat.

Another relative is spelt, a natural mating of durum and a common weed. Spelt is the delicious wheat used to make bread in Europe in the Middle Ages. An heirloom grain, it is still grown in areas along the Rhine and Danube Rivers, and has gained popularity among American bread makers.

A kernel of wheat is known as the five-in-one; it is about 11 percent protein, and contains carbohydrates, both soluble and insoluble fiber, vitamins, and minerals. The less it is processed, the more nutritious it is. Look for products with the germ intact: whole-wheat flours, wheat germ, and bran. White flours, semolina, farina, couscous, and bulgur are all processed wheat products and are low in fiber and high in starch.

Wheat comes in hard and soft varieties (based on the volume of gluten in the cells); planted in winter (sown in autumn and harvested in early summer) or spring (sown in spring and harvested in late summer, and containing more gluten); organic and stone-ground; as spelt (known as the bread wheats); as kamut and durum (known as the pasta wheats). There are all sorts of grinds and degrees of milled grains in between.

With fine grinds, all parts of the grain are equally ground; medium and coarse grinds have varying amounts of bran dispersed through the flour, which gives baked goods a slightly more crumbly texture. The finest grind of whole-wheat flour makes a moist, fine-textured bread that I find exceptionally appealing. Whole-wheat breads will always have a coarse, firm, rough texture and a dark brown color. Graham flour handles like any whole-wheat flour and has a fabulous extra-nutty flavor.

Spelt flour, kamut flour, and triticale flour can be used as an exact substitute for whole-wheat flours in baking recipes, although the flavors are deeper and richer, and textures will vary slightly. White whole-wheat flour makes pale golden breads with a sweet taste and light texture that end up halfway between whole-wheat and white breads.

Types of Products

Raw wheat berries are the hulled whole kernels. Use to make home-milled flours, or cooked or sprouted to make breads. Grains can be white, russet, purple, or amber in color. Spelt, kamut, and triticale are also available as whole grains.

Bread flour, also called high-protein flour, is ground from hard red spring wheat that has some malted barley added. It is unbleached; that is, aged without chemicals or preservatives. It has a protein content of 12 to 20 percent. High-gluten wheat absorbs more liquid than other flours and creates a more elastic dough and light-textured bread.

Unbleached all-purpose flour is perfectly good for making yeast breads and quick breads, being blended from a variety of wheats to an approximate combination of 80 percent hard wheat (14 percent gluten) and 20 percent soft (6 to 8 percent gluten). These percentages vary, depending on the brand and its origin. Unbleached all-purpose flour is aged for a few months

to oxidize the proteins and bleach out the natural light-yellow pigment present in freshly milled, or green, flour. Doughs made with this flour are more springy and elastic than if made from bleached flour, and the baked loaves are higher in volume.

Whole-wheat pastry flour, ground from low-gluten wheat, is used for tender biscuits, cakes, and pastry. It feels very silky smooth. It contains less gluten than white bread flours.

Whole-wheat flour is ground from the fiber-rich whole wheat berry, including the oil-rich bran and germ. A soft whole-wheat flour that makes great flatbreads is sold as tortilla flour in Hispanic markets.

Bolted flour is new to home bakers but well known to professionals. Marketed as Guisto's Old Mill Reduced Bran Flour, it is stone-ground and has 80 percent of the bran sifted out. It makes fabulous sandwich or country breads on its own or in combination with other whole-wheat flours such as spelt, kamut, and triticale. Make your own bolted flour by combining 3 cups unbleached white flour, 1 cup fine or medium stone-ground whole-wheat flour, and 3 tablespoons raw wheat germ.

White whole-wheat flour is a strain of finely ground light-hulled winter wheat grown in Kansas and Montana. It is especially sweet in flavor. White whole-wheat flour can be substituted for regular whole-wheat flours.

Semolina flour is the finely ground endosperm of cream-colored durum wheat. Used extensively for pasta, it makes a delicious, high-protein addition to Italian-style breads and can be used interchangeably with other wheat flours. Semolina flour is not the same as semolina meal, which is a coarse-ground wheat cereal, farina, used like coarse cornmeal.

Graham flour is a special grind of whole wheat popularized by health advocate Sylvester Graham in the late nineteenth century, when processed flours were becoming the norm. The bran and germ are quite coarse and the endosperm is ground very fine, giving the resulting flour a rich, unique nutty flavor. It can be used interchangeably with whole-wheat flour.

Spelt flour, made from unrefined and nutritious emmer wheat, has its own unique flavor and is easier to digest than regular whole-wheat flour. White spelt flour and whole grain spelt flour are available. In Europe, spelt is dried in kilns to give it a slightly smoky flavor.

Kamut flour is ground from Montana-grown wheat with near-transparent amber kernels. Related to durum wheat, it is high in protein and has a sweet aroma. Use ⅞ cup kamut flour for 1 cup whole-wheat flour and don't add other ingredients; doughs made with kamut are slow risers, like those made with semolina.

Gluten flour is made by washing about 30 percent of the starch from the endosperm of high-protein hard wheat. What remains is a flour high in protein and low in starch and sodium. It is called for in special diet breads and as a protein booster in low- and nongluten whole-grain flour doughs, like rye and barley. Loaves made with all gluten flour have a reputation for being tough.

Vital wheat gluten, even more concentrated than gluten flour, has had about 70 percent of the starch removed. Adding 1½ teaspoons vital wheat gluten for every 1 cup specialty flour is necessary for achieving loaves that have a light, springy texture. This is the form of gluten called for in bread machine recipes and in recipes calling simply for gluten. Do not confuse vital wheat gluten and gluten flour.

Triticale flour is a finely ground hybrid of wheat and rye. It tastes more like rye, but has a low gluten content similar to wheat. Although triticale handles and rises like whole wheat, it is best used in a one-to-one ratio with wheat flour.

Cake flour is bleached white pastry flour. It is not used for baking breads. Because it contains six to eight percent protein and is milled very fine, cake flour is best for biscuits, muffins, cakes, and pastries. Never use "instant" flour unless specifically called for in a recipe. It is not interchangeable with cake flour, but is used for sauces and gravies.

Self-rising flour contains leavening in the form of bicarbonate of soda and salt. It is favored for baking southern-style biscuits and cannot be substituted for cake flour.

Rolled wheat flakes are wheat berries that have been steamed and rolled flat. They are used like rolled oats and barley.

Cracked wheat is a fine, medium, or coarse cut of the wheat kernel with the bran removed. It is different from bulgur wheat, which is parboiled and dried. Couscous, cracked durum wheat, is a good substitute.

Wheat germ is the embryo, or heart, of the wheat berry. It has a high oil content and must be stored in the refrigerator. Available raw, toasted, and with honey, it is added to bread to boost fiber and nutrition.

Wheat bran, the outer layer of the wheat berry, adds color, nutrition, and fiber to breads. Soak first in hot water to soften. It is also marketed as unprocessed wheat bran or miller's bran.

Of all the whole-wheat flours, coarse-ground graham flour probably has the most nostalgic associations. My grandmother's generation used this favorite grind of extra-nutty wheat flour whenever they could get it.

Graham Biscuits

Makes 24 biscuits

3 tablespoons graham flour, for sprinkling

3 tablespoons wheat germ, for sprinkling

1½ cups unbleached all-purpose flour

1½ cups graham flour

2 tablespoons baking powder

1 teaspoon cream of tartar

1 teaspoon salt

½ cup (1 stick) unsalted butter, chilled and cut into pieces

2 large eggs, lightly beaten

1 cup cold milk or heavy cream, plus 2 tablespoons for brushing

2 tablespoons poppy seeds

1. Preheat an oven to 425°F and position a rack in the center of the oven. Grease a baking sheet or line with parchment paper. Sprinkle with the 3 tablespoons graham flour and the wheat germ.

2. In a bowl, combine the all-purpose and 1½ cups graham flours, baking powder, cream of tartar, and salt. Cut the butter into the dry ingredients with a pastry blender or 2 knives until the mixture resembles coarse crumbs and no large chunks of butter remain. If the butter gets very soft, refrigerate the mixture for 20 minutes to rechill. Add the eggs and milk, stirring until the ingredients are just moistened. The dough will be slightly shaggy, moist and a bit stiff but not sticky.

3. Turn the dough out onto a lightly floured work surface. Knead gently until the dough just holds together, about 10 times. Pat the dough into a rectangle 1 inch thick. Cut with a sharp knife or pastry wheel, making 6 squares across and 4 down to make 24 small squares in all. Brush biscuits lightly with milk or cream and sprinkle with poppy seeds. Arrange, at least ½ inch apart, on the prepared sheet.

4. Bake for 15 to 18 minutes, or until golden brown. Let rest for a few minutes and serve hot, although they can also be eaten at room temperature.

Breads with sprouted grains have been tremendously popular with bakers for decades. The wheat berries add texture and nutrition to this light whole-wheat and honey bread. Sprouting the grain takes a few days, but is a simple process.

Sprouted Wheat Bread

Makes three 8-by-4-inch loaves

½ cup warm water (105° to 115°F)

1½ tablespoons (1½ packages) active dry yeast

Pinch of sugar

Pinch of ground ginger

2 cups whole-wheat flour

1 cup nonfat dry milk powder

1 tablespoon salt

1½ cups warm water (105° to 115°F)

¼ cup honey

4 tablespoons (½ stick) unsalted butter, at room temperature

2 cups sprouted wheat berries, chopped (recipe follows)

4½ to 5 cups bread flour

Wheat germ, for sprinkling

Melted butter, for brushing

1. Pour the ½ cup warm water into a small bowl. Sprinkle the yeast, sugar, and ginger over the water. Stir to dissolve and let stand until foamy, about 10 minutes.

2. In a large bowl using a whisk or in the bowl of a heavy-duty electric mixer fitted with the paddle attachment, combine the whole-wheat flour, milk powder, and salt. Add the warm water, honey, and 4 tablespoons butter. Beat for 1 minute. Add the yeast mixture and beat 1 minute longer. Add all the wheat berries and the bread flour, ½ cup at a time, beating on low speed until a soft dough that just clears the sides of the bowl forms, switching to a wooden spoon when necessary if making by hand.

3. Turn the dough out onto a lightly floured work surface and knead until soft and spongy, 1 to 2 minutes for a machine-mixed dough and 3 to 4 minutes for a hand-mixed dough, dusting with flour only 1 tablespoon at a time, just enough as needed to prevent sticking. Place in a lightly greased deep container, turn once to coat the top, and cover with plastic wrap. Let rise at room temperature until double in bulk, 1½ to 2 hours.

4. Grease three 8-by-4-inch loaf pans and sprinkle the bottom and sides with wheat germ. Turn the dough out onto the work surface and divide into 3 equal portions. Pat each portion into a rectangle and roll into a loaf shape. Place, seam side down, into the prepared pans. Cover loosely with plastic wrap and let rise until level with the rims of the pans, about 1 hour.

5. About 20 minutes before baking, preheat an oven to 350°F and position a rack in the center of the oven.

6. Bake for 45 to 50 minutes, or until crusty and golden. Brush the tops with melted butter. Remove from the pans to cool on a rack.

continued

Sprouted Wheat Berries

Makes 2 cups

½ cup raw wheat berries

Place the wheat berries in a bowl and add tepid water to cover by 1 inch. Let stand at room temperature for 6 to 8 hours. Drain the wheat berries and rinse with fresh water. Divide between two 1-quart jars. Cover with cheesecloth and secure with a rubber band. Place the jars on their sides in a warm, dark place. Twice a day, rinse and drain the wheat berries with tepid water poured through the cheesecloth. After 2 to 3 days, the wheat berries will sprout. Refrigerate in a plastic bag for up to 3 days. Grind in a food processor fitted with the metal blade. Do not overprocess; the berries should be chunky.

Bread-Machine Sprouted Wheat Bread

1½-pound loaf

1 cup plus 2 tablespoons water

2 tablespoons unsalted butter, melted

3 tablespoons honey

2¼ cups bread flour

1 cup whole-wheat flour

⅓ cup nonfat dry milk powder

4 teaspoons vital wheat gluten

1¼ teaspoons salt

2½ teaspoons bread machine yeast

¾ cup sprouted wheat berries (previous page), chopped

1-pound loaf

¾ cup water

1½ tablespoons unsalted butter, melted

2 tablespoons honey

1½ cups bread flour

¾ cup whole-wheat flour

¼ cup nonfat dry milk powder

3 teaspoons vital wheat gluten

¾ teaspoon salt

2 teaspoons bread machine yeast

½ cup sprouted wheat berries (previous page), chopped

1. Place all the ingredients, except the sprouted wheat berries, in the pan according to the manufacturer's instructions. Set crust on medium and program for the basic or whole-wheat bread cycle; press Start. At the beep or at the end of the first kneading, add the chopped sprouted berries. Do not add extra liquid to the dough until after adding the wheat berries, as they add some moisture.

2. After the baking cycle ends, remove the bread from the pan and place on a rack to cool.

For this excellent loaf, use the creamy-colored semolina flour milled for pasta making, not the coarse variety also known as farina. You can also substitute canary-yellow durum flour, which contains the bran and germ. The bread is wonderful, especially with garlic butter.

Sesame Semolina Bread

Makes two 9-by-5-inch loaves

Sponge

1 tablespoon (1 package) active dry yeast

3 cups warm water (100°F)

2 cups semolina flour

2 cups bread flour

Dough

1 tablespoon salt

3 tablespoons good-quality olive oil

1 cup semolina flour

2½ to 3 cups bread flour

2 tablespoons farina, for sprinkling

1 egg beaten with 1 teaspoon water, for brushing

¼ cup sesame seeds, for sprinkling

3 tablespoons olive oil, for drizzling

1. **To make the sponge:** In a large bowl using a whisk or in the bowl of a heavy-duty electric mixer fitted with the paddle attachment, combine the yeast, warm water, and semolina and bread flours. Beat hard until smooth, about 30 seconds. Cover loosely with plastic wrap and let rise at room temperature until bubbly and at least double in bulk, about 3 hours.

2. **To prepare the dough:** Add the salt, olive oil, semolina flour, and ½ cup of the bread flour to the sponge. Beat until smooth, 1 minute. Add the remaining bread flour, ½ cup at a time, beating on low speed until a soft dough that just clears the sides of the bowl forms, switching to a wooden spoon when necessary if making by hand.

3. Turn the dough out onto a lightly floured work surface and knead vigorously until the dough is springy and smooth, 1 to 2 minutes for a machine-mixed dough and 3 to 4 minutes for a hand-mixed dough, dusting with flour only 1 tablespoon at a time, just enough as needed to prevent sticking. The dough should be soft, yet not sticky, and able to hold its shape. Place in a lightly greased deep container, brush lightly with olive oil, turn once to coat the top, and cover with plastic wrap. Let rise at room temperature until triple in bulk, 2 to 3 hours.

4. Grease two 9-by-5-inch loaf pans and sprinkle with the farina. Turn the dough out onto a clean work surface and divide into 2 equal portions. Pat each portion into a rectangle and roll into a loaf shape. Place, seam side down, in the prepared pans. Cover loosely with plastic wrap and let rise until almost double in bulk, about 1 hour.

5. About 20 minutes before baking, preheat an oven to 425°F and position a rack in the center of the oven.

6. Gently brush both loaves with the egg and water mixture and sprinkle generously with the sesame seeds. Using a sharp knife, make a slash about ½ inch deep along the length of each loaf. Drizzle the slashes with the 3 tablespoons olive oil. Bake for 15 minutes, then reduce the oven temperature to 375°F and bake for 25 to 30 minutes longer, or until golden brown and crusty. Remove from the pans to cool on a rack.

Bread-Machine Sesame Semolina Bread

1½-pound loaf

1⅓ cups water

2 tablespoons good-quality olive oil

1 tablespoon sugar

1½ cups unbleached bread flour

1½ cups semolina flour

1½ tablespoons sesame seeds

3 teaspoons vital wheat gluten

1 teaspoon salt

1¾ teaspoons bread machine yeast

1-pound loaf

1 cup water

1½ tablespoons good-quality olive oil

2 teaspoons sugar

1 cup unbleached bread flour

1 cup semolina flour

1 tablespoon sesame seeds

2 teaspoons vital wheat gluten

¾ teaspoon salt

1¼ teaspoons bread machine yeast

1. Place all of the ingredients in the pan according to the manufacturer's instructions. Set crust on medium and program for the basic bread cycle; press Start.

2. After the baking cycle ends, remove the bread from the pan and place on a rack to cool.

This bread has an airy, open texture and pale tawny-brown color. The thick crust is hard and crisp right after baking, but softens as the bread cools. For best flavor and texture, serve the baguettes within a few hours of baking.

Kamut Baguettes

Makes 4 baguettes

2½ cups warm water (105° to 115°F)

1½ tablespoons (2 packages) active dry yeast

2 tablespoons sugar

2 tablespoons unsalted butter, melted

1 tablespoon salt

3½ cups kamut flour

About 3 cups bread flour

Yellow cornmeal or farina, for dusting

1 egg white beaten with 1 tablespoon water, for glaze

1. Pour ½ cup of the warm water into a small bowl. Sprinkle the yeast and a pinch of the sugar over the water. Stir to dissolve and let stand at room temperature until foamy, about 10 minutes.

2. In a large bowl using a whisk or in the bowl of a heavy-duty electric mixer fitted with the paddle attachment, combine the remaining 2 cups warm water, remaining sugar, butter, salt, 1 cup of the kamut flour, and 1 cup of the bread flour. Beat hard until creamy, about 1 minute. Stir in the yeast mixture and remaining kamut flour; beat hard for 2 minutes. Add the remaining bread flour, ½ cup at a time, beating on low speed until a soft, shaggy dough that just clears the sides of the bowl forms, switching to a wooden spoon when necessary if making by hand.

3. Turn the dough out onto a lightly floured work surface and knead until soft and springy, 1 to 3 minutes for a machine-mixed dough and 3 to 6 minutes for a hand-mixed dough, dusting with flour only 1 tablespoon at a time, just enough as needed to prevent sticking. Do not add too much flour, or the dough will stiffen up. Place in a greased deep container, sprinkle the top with flour, and cover with plastic wrap. Let rise

continued

at room temperature until double in bulk, 2 to
3 hours. Do not rush.

4. Grease 2 baking sheets or line with parchment
paper, or grease two 16-by-9-by-2-inch baguette pans.
Dust with cornmeal. Turn the dough out onto a clean
work surface and divide into 4 equal portions. Using
your palm, pat each portion into a thin 14-by-6-inch
rectangle. Starting at a long end, roll each rectangle,
using your thumbs to help roll tightly. Using the side
of your hand, create a depression lengthwise down
the center of each loaf. Fold lengthwise and pinch the
seams to seal. Roll back and forth from the center out
to adjust the dough in a tight cylinder slightly shorter
than the baking sheet. Gently transfer, seam side down,
to the prepared sheets. Cover loosely with plastic wrap
and let rise until the dough is double in bulk, about
1 hour.

5. About 20 minutes before baking, preheat an oven to
425°F and position a rack in the middle of the oven.

6. Brush the loaves with the egg glaze. Using a sharp
knife, make 3 or 4 diagonal slashes no more than
¼ inch deep down the top center of each loaf. Just
before baking, mist the oven a few times with water,
if desired. Place the sheets in the oven and reduce
the oven temperature to 375°F. If desired, after 15 minutes, spray the loaves quickly to create steam, without
pulling the rack out of the oven and taking care to
protect your hands from burning. Repeat two more
times at 5-minute intervals. Bake for a total of 30 to
35 minutes, or until the loaves are deep brown and
sound hollow when tapped with your finger. If both
sheets do not fit into the oven at one time, bake one
at a time. Remove the loaves from the sheets to cool
on a rack.

Bread-Machine Kamut Baguettes

1½-pound loaf

1¼ cups water

1½ cups bread flour

1⅔ cups kamut flour

4 teaspoons vital wheat gluten

1 tablespoon sugar

1 teaspoon salt

2 teaspoons bread machine yeast

1-pound loaf

¾ cup water

1 cup bread flour

1 cup kamut flour

3 teaspoons vital wheat gluten

2 teaspoons sugar

½ teaspoon salt

1½ teaspoons bread machine yeast

1. Place the ingredients in the pan according to the manufacturer's instructions. Set crust on medium and program for French bread cycle; press Start. After the kneading cycle, reset, allowing the dough to be kneaded a second time.

2. After the baking cycle ends, remove the bread from the pan and place on a rack to cool.

This rich-textured, dense whole-grain bread should be kneaded with a light, gentle hand, as the gluten in the dough is more delicate than in its rye and whole-wheat cousins. Triticale flour needs only one rest period and is a slow riser. As the title suggests, the bread is great toasted and spread with maple butter.

Triticale Toasting Bread

Makes two 8-by-4-inch loaves

Sponge

1½ tablespoons (1½ packages) active dry yeast

2 cups triticale flour

¼ cup honey

¾ cup tepid water (100°F)

1½ cups milk, at room temperature

Dough

¼ cup vegetable oil

2 teaspoons salt

3½ to 4 cups bread flour

2 tablespoons unsalted butter, melted, for brushing

Spiced Maple Butter (recipe follows)

1. **To make the sponge:** In a large bowl using a whisk or in the bowl of a heavy-duty electric mixer fitted with the whisk attachment, combine the yeast, triticale flour, honey, tepid water, and milk. Beat hard until smooth and creamy. Cover loosely with plastic wrap and let stand at room temperature for about 1 hour, or until bubbly.

2. **To make the dough:** Add the oil, salt, and 1 cup of the bread flour to the sponge and stir with a wooden spoon or the paddle attachment to combine. Beat for 1 minute. Add the remaining bread flour, ½ cup at a time, beating on low speed until a soft, shaggy dough that just clears the sides of the bowl forms.

3. Turn the dough out onto a lightly floured work surface and gently knead until the dough is rather soft and sticky, but is elastic and holds its shape, 1 minute for a machine-mixed dough and 2 minutes for a hand-mixed dough, dusting with flour only 1 tablespoon at a time, just enough to prevent sticking. Cover with a clean kitchen towel and let stand for 15 minutes.

4. Grease the bottom and sides of two 8-by-4-inch loaf pans (I like to use terra-cotta pans). Divide the dough

continued

into 2 equal portions. Pat each portion into a rectangular shape and roll into a loaf shape. Place the loaves, seam side down, into the prepared pans. Cover loosely with plastic wrap and let rise until the dough is puffy and about 1 inch above the rims of the pans, about 1¼ hours.

5. About 20 minutes before baking, preheat an oven to 375°F and position a rack in the center of the oven.

6. Brush the top of each loaf with melted butter. Using a sharp knife, make a long horizontal slash no more than ¼ inch deep down the top center. Drizzle the slash with melted butter. Bake for 40 to 45 minutes, or until the tops are deep brown, the sides slightly contract from the pan, and the loaves sound hollow when tapped with your finger. Remove from the pans to cool on a rack. Serve with Spiced Maple Butter.

Spiced Maple Butter

Makes about ½ cup

½ cup (1 stick) unsalted butter, at room temperature, cut into pieces

2 tablespoons pure maple syrup

½ teaspoon ground cinnamon

In a small bowl, cream the butter, maple syrup, and cinnamon, using a wooden spoon or handheld electric mixer, until smooth. Transfer to a small container, cover, and refrigerate until serving. Store in the refrigerator for up to 2 months.

A version of this divine loaf is baked by the nuns at a cloistered convent located in the unlikely site of Hollywood, California. Carob is the sweet inner flesh of the pods of an evergreen tree, which is ground to a powder. Another unlikely substitute for flour in hard times, it was supposedly eaten by Christ during his sojourn in the wilderness.

Monastery of the Angels Brown Bread

Makes two 8-by-4-inch loaves

2¼ cups warm water (105° to 115°F)

1½ tablespoons (1½ packages) active dry yeast

Pinch of packed light brown sugar or raw sugar

3 tablespoons unsalted butter, melted

¼ cup packed light brown sugar or raw sugar

¼ cup carob powder

½ cup nonfat dry milk powder

3 tablespoons sesame seeds

1 tablespoon salt

1 cup bread flour

4 to 4½ cups whole-wheat flour

1 egg beaten with 1 teaspoon water, for glaze

1. Pour ½ cup of the warm water into a small bowl. Sprinkle the yeast and pinch of sugar over the water. Stir to dissolve and let stand at room temperature until foamy, about 10 minutes.

2. In a large bowl using a whisk or in the bowl of a heavy-duty electric mixer fitted with the paddle attachment, combine the remaining 1¾ cups warm water, butter, ¼ cup sugar, carob, milk powder, sesame seeds, salt, bread flour, and ½ cup of the whole-wheat flour. Beat until smooth, about 1 minute. Add the yeast mixture and beat vigorously for 2 minutes longer. Add the remaining whole-wheat flour, ½ cup at a time, beating on low speed until a soft dough that just clears the sides of the bowl forms, switching to a wooden spoon when necessary if making by hand. Keep this dough soft, as it stiffens up easily.

3. Turn the dough out onto a lightly floured work surface and knead until smooth and elastic, 1 to 2 minutes for a machine-mixed dough and 4 to 6 minutes for a hand-mixed dough, dusting with flour only 1 tablespoon at a time, just enough as needed to prevent sticking. Place in a lightly greased deep container, turn once to coat the top, and cover with plastic wrap. Let rise at

room temperature until double in bulk, 1½ to 2 hours. Gently deflate and let rise again for 30 minutes.

4. Lightly grease the bottom and sides of two 8-by-4-inch loaf pans. Turn the dough out onto the work surface and divide into 2 equal portions. Pat each portion into a rectangle and roll into a loaf shape. Place the loaves, seam side down, into the prepared pans. Cover loosely with plastic wrap and let rise until double in bulk and about 1 inch above the rims of the pans, 30 to 45 minutes.

5. About 20 minutes before baking, preheat an oven to 375°F and position a rack in the center of the oven.

6. Using a sharp knife, make a slash about ½ inch deep along the entire length of each loaf. Brush with the egg and water glaze. Bake for 40 to 45 minutes, or until the tops are golden brown, the sides slightly contract from the pan, and the loaves sound hollow when tapped with your finger. Remove from the pans to cool on a rack.

This wholesome loaf is sweet and nutty. It is a perfect begin-ning loaf using whole-grain spelt flour, plus eggs for extra leavening. To help the dough retain moisture, cover with plastic wrap during all risings. The sandwich buns are great for burgers and sandwiches.

Whole-Grain Spelt Egg Bread

Makes 2 free-form loaves or 20 sandwich buns

2 cups warm water (105° to 115°F)

2 tablespoons (2 packages) active dry yeast

Pinch of sugar

7 tablespoons unsalted butter, melted

½ cup light molasses

1 tablespoon salt

3 large eggs

3 cups bread flour

3½ to 4 cups whole-grain spelt flour

Melted butter or olive oil, for brushing

1. Pour ½ cup of the warm water into a small bowl. Sprinkle the yeast and sugar over the water. Stir to dis-solve and let stand at room temperature until foamy, about 10 minutes.

2. In a large bowl using a whisk or in the bowl of a heavy-duty electric mixer fitted with the paddle attach-ment, combine the remaining 1½ cups warm water, melted butter, molasses, salt, eggs, and bread flour. Beat hard until creamy, about 1 minute. Stir in the yeast mixture. Add the spelt flour, ½ cup at a time, beating for 1 minute on low speed after adding 2 cups, switch-ing to a wooden spoon when necessary if making by hand. Continue adding the flour, ½ cup at a time, until a soft, shaggy dough that just clears the sides of the bowl forms.

3. Turn the dough out onto a lightly floured work sur-face and knead until soft and springy, 1 to 3 minutes for a machine-mixed dough and 4 to 7 minutes for a hand-mixed dough, dusting with flour only 1 table-spoon at a time, just enough as needed to prevent sticking. The dough will have a slightly rough surface and feel sticky, but not dry. Do not add too much flour or the loaves will be dry and crumbly. Place in a lightly greased deep container, turn once to coat the top, and cover with plastic wrap. Let rise at room temperature

until double in bulk, about 1½ hours. Do not allow this bread to rise any higher, or it may collapse and bake into a flat loaf.

4. Return the dough to the mixing bowl and beat with a wooden spoon or the dough hook for 2 minutes. Grease a baking sheet or line with parchment paper. Turn the dough out onto a lightly floured work surface and divide into 6 equal portions. With the palms of your hands, roll into 6 ropes, each about 12 inches long. Place 3 of the ropes side by side and braid. Tuck the ends under and pinch to seal. Repeat to form the second loaf. Place on the prepared sheet. Brush the tops with melted butter. Cover loosely with plastic wrap and let rise until the dough is puffy, about 30 minutes.

5. About 20 minutes before baking, preheat an oven to 400°F and position a rack in the center of the oven.

6. Brush the tops again with butter. Bake for 10 minutes, then reduce the oven temperature to 350°F and bake for 25 to 30 minutes longer, or until the tops are golden brown and the loaves sound hollow when tapped with your finger. Remove from the sheet to cool on a rack.

Spelt Sandwich Buns:

Grease 2 baking sheets or line with parchment paper. After the first rising, turn the dough out onto the work surface and divide into 20 equal portions. Roll each portion with a cupped hand into a tight round ball. Place, seam side down and at least 2 inches apart, on the prepared baking sheets. Flatten each ball into a 1-inch-high disk with your palm. Cover loosely with plastic wrap and let rise until puffy, about 20 minutes. Preheat an oven to 375°F and position a rack in the center of the oven. Bake for 20 to 25 minutes, or until slightly brown and firm to the touch. Remove from the sheets to cool on a rack.

Wild Rice

Wild rice, the folkloric state grain of Minnesota, is known as a gourmet or epicurean grain. Not a rice or a true grain, it is tall, slender, ornamental aquatic grass, growing about twelve feet high. It is the only grain-like crop native to North America, growing in the lakes and shallow moving waters along the American-Canadian border.

Early Native Americans called wild rice *mahnon-men. Mano* means "good," and *min,* "berry." The word signifies "gift from the creator." Wild rice was grown in the Great Lakes region, mainly by Chippewa (Ojibwa) and Algonquin- and Siouan-speaking tribes clustered around Lake Superior.

Seventeenth-century French fur traders, and the Jesuit missionaries who followed, adopted wild rice into their diets and called this staple food "crazy oats." It was dubbed "Indian rice" and then "Tuscarora rice" after the Iroquois name for wild rice, *tuskaro.* The name later evolved to wild rice, since the grains are long like white rice and the plant requires aquatic culture.

Some wild rice is still harvested in the traditional way by Native Americans. Balancing in canoes, they beat the spikes with flexible forked flails cut from saplings. The green rice is then parched in cast-iron kettles over wood fires. All wild rice must be parched or roasted first to reduce the moisture, deepen the color, and develop the flavor.

Since paddy-raised wild rice must be harvested in one sweep, a strain had to be developed to fit large-scale commercial production needs. In 1972, pioneer Harold Kosbau planted the first man-made paddies in Minnesota, and much of today's wild rice crop is cultivated in California, Minnesota, Idaho, and Canada. Native Americans claim that paddy rice is quite different, especially in flavor. It constitutes 80 percent of all wild rice sold. The next big step was for traditional harvesters to use airboats in lieu of canoes.

Hand-gathered lake rice, always labeled with its place of origin, is still quite expensive, but cultivated rice is very affordable. The color of the rice also indicates how it was grown. Hand-harvested rice is distinctly matte; paddy rice is a very shiny sable-black. Paddy rice is left to cure out in the weather, resulting in the characteristic shiny, dark kernels, while hand-harvested rice is parched immediately over open fires, giving it a variety of matte colors from ruddy red-brown, deep chocolate, and tan to subtle gray-green. Use cultivated rice (also known as "tame rice") or hand-harvested rice (known as "real rice") interchangeably for bread baking.

Wild rice is equal nutritionally to oat groats, and the bran is a good source of insoluble fiber. It has plenty of protein (more than wheat, but still incomplete), lysine, and B vitamins, as well as zinc, iron, potassium, and copper.

Wild rice has an earthy, smoky-rich, nutty flavor, much like black tea. The darker the rice, the stronger the flavor. Each brand has its own particular taste, so if you have experienced a brand that was too husky or bitter for your palate, experiment with other brands or use in combination with other rices for a milder taste. When cooked, the grains swell and split slightly down the side to reveal a grayish interior. If the grains split and curl, they are overcooked. Larger grains need longer cooking than smaller ones; broken grains, found in many packages, cook the quickest.

Use one to two cups cooked wild rice per six cups wheat flour for the best results in bread. Use wild rice flour sparingly—no more than one cup wild rice flour to five cups wheat flour—as it has no gluten.

Types of Products

Wild rice comes in three grades: select, which contains short and broken grains; extra-fancy, uniform medium grains about ½ inch long; and giant, grains 1 inch in length and considered the premium long grade. All grades can be used interchangeably in bread recipes, but must be cooked first.

Wild rice flour is finely ground from the whole grain. It is easily ground in a coffee grinder to a fine powder.

Wild rice is a perfect complement to oatmeal and molasses. This loaf is rich and moist.

Wild Rice Bread with Sunflower Seeds

Makes 3 large round loaves

2 cups water

1 cup wild rice

1 cup warm milk (105° to 115°F)

1½ tablespoons (1½ packages) active dry yeast

Pinch of sugar

2 cups warm water (105° to 115°F)

1 cup quick-cooking oatmeal

¾ cup light molasses

¼ cup sunflower seed oil, plus oil for brushing

1 tablespoon salt

7 to 7½ cups bread flour

1¼ cups raw sunflower seeds

1 egg, beaten, for glaze

1. In a saucepan, bring the water to a rolling boil. Add the rice, return to a boil, reduce the heat to the lowest setting, cover, and cook until tender and fluffy and all the liquid has been absorbed, 30 to 35 minutes for hand-harvested rice and 50 to 55 minutes for paddy-grown rice. The rice should be slightly underdone. You should have 1½ cups. Spread on a baking sheet and set aside to cool.

2. Pour the warm milk into a small bowl. Sprinkle the yeast and sugar over the milk. Stir to dissolve and let stand until foamy, about 10 minutes.

3. In a large bowl using a whisk or in the bowl of a heavy-duty electric mixer fitted with the paddle attachment, combine the water, oatmeal, molasses, ¼ cup oil, and wild rice. Add the salt and 2 cups of the bread flour. Add the yeast mixture and ¾ cup of the sunflower seeds; beat hard until smooth, about 1 minute. Continue to add the bread flour, ½ cup at a time, beating on low speed until a soft dough that just clears the sides of the bowl forms, switching to a wooden spoon when necessary if making by hand.

4. Turn the dough out onto a well-floured work surface and knead until dense, yet still quite soft and springy,

continued

1 to 2 minutes for a machine-mixed dough and 3 to 4 minutes for a hand-mixed dough, dusting with flour only 1 tablespoon at a time, just enough as needed to prevent sticking. Place in a lightly greased deep container, turn once to coat the top, and cover with plastic wrap. Let rise at room temperature until double in bulk, 2 to 2½ hours. Do not worry if rising takes a bit longer.

5. Grease a baking sheet or line with parchment paper. Turn the dough out onto a lightly floured work surface and divide into 3 equal portions. Form each portion into a round loaf and place on the prepared sheet. Brush the tops with sunflower seed oil and cover loosely with plastic wrap. Let rise until double in bulk, about 1 hour.

6. About 20 minutes before baking, preheat an oven to 350°F and position a rack in the center of the oven.

7. Brush the tops of the loaves with the beaten egg and sprinkle with the remaining ½ cup sunflower seeds. Bake for 40 to 45 minutes, or until the loaves are browned and sound hollow when tapped with a finger. Remove from the sheet to cool on a rack.

To cook the wild rice, please follow the instructions on page 134. For the 1½ pound loaf, use ⅔ cup water and ⅓ raw wild rice. For the 1 pound loaf, use ½ cup water and ¼ cup raw rice.

Bread-Machine Wild Rice Bread with Sunflower Seeds

1½-pound loaf	1-pound loaf
1¼ cups water	⅞ cup water
¼ cup sunflower seed oil	3 tablespoons sunflower seed oil
¼ cup molasses	3 tablespoons molasses
2¾ cups bread flour	2 cups bread flour
⅓ cup rolled oats	¼ cup rolled oats
3 tablespoons nonfat dry milk	2 tablespoons nonfat dry milk
4 teaspoons vital wheat gluten	2½ teaspoons vital wheat gluten
1 teaspoon salt	¾ teaspoon salt
1¾ teaspoons bread machine yeast	1¼ teaspoons bread machine yeast
⅔ cup cooked wild rice (see page 134)	½ cup cooked wild rice (see page 134)
¼ cup sunflower seeds	3 tablespoons sunflower seeds

1. Place the ingredients, except the wild rice and sunflower seeds, in the pan according to the manufacturer's instructions. Set crust on medium and program for the fruit and nut bread cycle; press Start. At the beep, remove the dough and knead in the wild rice and seeds by hand. Return the dough to the pan and continue the cycle.

2. After the baking cycle ends, remove the bread from the pan and place on a rack to cool.

Adapted from a dish on the menu of a New England bed-and-breakfast inn, these pancakes are delicious served in a stack with a dollop of Maple Cranberry Butter placed on top and allowed to melt down the sides.

Buckwheat Wild Rice Pancakes

Makes about sixteen 4-inch pancakes

1½ cups unbleached all-purpose flour

¾ cup light buckwheat flour

2 teaspoons baking powder

1 teaspoon baking soda

½ teaspoon salt

2 cups buttermilk

1⅓ cups cold cooked wild rice (see page 134)

4 tablespoons (½ stick) butter or margarine, melted

4 large eggs

   Maple Cranberry Butter (recipe follows)

1. In a large bowl, combine the all-purpose and buckwheat flours, baking powder, baking soda, and salt. In another bowl, whisk together the buttermilk, wild rice, butter, and eggs. Add to the dry ingredients, stirring until just combined. Do not overmix; the batter will have small lumps and be thick.

2. Heat a griddle or heavy skillet over medium heat until drops of water sprinkled on the surface dance over it, then lightly grease. Using a ¼-cup measure for each pancake, pour the batter onto the griddle. Cook until bubbles form on the surface, the edges are dry, and the bottoms are golden brown, about 2 minutes. Turn once. The second side will take about 1 minute to cook. Serve at once with Maple Cranberry Butter.

Maple Cranberry Butter

Makes about 2 cups

1 cup (2 sticks) unsalted butter, at room temperature, cut into pieces

¼ cup pure maple syrup

1 cup whole-berry cranberry sauce

In a small bowl, beat the butter and maple syrup just until fluffy and light, using a wooden spoon or electric mixer. Add the cranberry sauce and beat until well blended. Serve at room temperature. Store, covered, in the refrigerator for up to 1 week.

These buttermilk biscuits have the classic proportions of dry ingredients to wet. The biscuits bake up high and delicate. To cook the wild rice, use the proportions of rice and water for Wild Rice Bread with Sunflower Seeds (page 134) and follow the instructions in step one.

Wild Rice Buttermilk Biscuits

Makes about twelve 2½-inch biscuits

2½ cups whole-wheat pastry flour

2 teaspoons baking powder

½ teaspoon baking soda

½ teaspoon salt

½ cup (1 stick) unsalted butter or margarine, cut into pieces

2 large eggs

1 cup cooked wild rice (see page 134)

⅓ to ½ cup buttermilk

About ¼ cup sesame seeds, for sprinkling

1. Preheat an oven to 425°F and position a rack in the center of the oven. Grease a baking sheet or line with parchment paper.

2. In a bowl, combine the flour, baking powder, baking soda, and salt. Cut the butter into the dry ingredients with a pastry blender or 2 knives until the mixture resembles coarse crumbs and no large chunks of butter remain. If the butter gets very soft, refrigerate the mixture for 20 minutes. Add the eggs, wild rice, and buttermilk, stirring until the ingredients are just moistened. The dough will be slightly shaggy, but not sticky.

3. Turn the dough out onto a lightly floured work surface. Knead gently until the dough just holds together, about 10 times. Sprinkle the work surface with flour and liberally sprinkle with half of the sesame seeds. Place the dough on the sesame seeds and pat into a rectangle ¾ inch thick; sprinkle the top of the dough with sesame seeds. Using a 2½-inch biscuit cutter dipped in flour, press firmly without twisting to make biscuits; the sesame seeds will coat the top and bottom crusts. Cut out biscuits as close together as possible for a minimum of leftover dough. Press the scraps gently together and cut out additional biscuits, sprinkling the work surface and dough with more sesame seeds. Place, ½ inch apart, on the prepared sheet.

4. Bake for 12 to 15 minutes, or until golden brown. Let rest for a few minutes and serve hot.

Specialty Flours

Specialty flours are used to make a variety of delicious yeast breads, flatbreads, and quick breads. Because they lack gluten, they must be used with wheat flour for a traditionally textured yeast bread. Use a one-to-four or one-to-five ratio, or one cup specialty flour to four or five cups wheat flour.

Chestnut

Chestnuts are sweet, starchy, very low-fat nuts from the beech tree family with a tough outer shell. High in carbohydrates, they have long been used as a substitute for bread throughout the Mediterranean. In that region, the chestnut tree was erstwhile known as the "bread tree," and its nuts were pounded by hand into flour with a club studded with nails. Imported Italian chestnut flour, ground from roasted nuts, is fast becoming a popular specialty flour. I consider it the most sensuous of all flours. Ground from dried chestnuts, it is sweet and nutty in flavor, yet divinely silky in texture.

Europeans and Asians are much more familiar with chestnut flour than Americans. In Tuscany, a famous dessert known as *castagnaccio* is made from chestnut flour, pine nuts, and raisins cooked in olive oil and is served with scoops of fresh ricotta cheese like a pancake. In Liguria on the Italian Riviera, a chestnut flatbread is baked on chestnut leaves placed on an earthenware platter.

Chestnut flour is a pretty beige to taupe in color. It must be stored in the refrigerator or freezer for freshness, as it is highly perishable. It has no gluten, so it must be paired in a small proportion with wheat flour to produce a delicate, distinctly flavored yeast bread.

The combination of chestnut flour and white whole-wheat flour makes for a smooth-textured, exceptionally flavored bread. This recipe is based on a loaf described by my baker-friend Lou Pappas, who is famous for using hazelnuts in her bread baking. It is great with St. Andrè cheese, sliced Black Forest ham, and a good white wine such as a Sauvignon Blanc.

Chestnut Bread with Hazelnuts

Makes two 8½-by-4½-inch loaves

1 cup warm water (105° to 115°F)

2 tablespoons (2 packages) active dry yeast

Pinch of brown sugar or a few drops of honey

1 cup warm milk (105° to 115°F)

2 tablespoons honey

¼ cup olive oil

1 tablespoon salt

½ cup chestnut flour

2 cups white whole-wheat flour

2½ to 3 cups bread flour

1 cup whole hazelnuts

1. Pour ½ cup of the warm water into a small bowl. Sprinkle the yeast and sugar over the water. Stir to dissolve and let stand at room temperature until foamy, about 10 minutes.

2. In a large bowl using a whisk or in the bowl of a heavy-duty electric mixer fitted with the paddle attachment, combine the remaining ½ cup warm water, milk, honey, oil, salt, and chestnut and whole-wheat flours. Add the yeast mixture. Beat until smooth, about 2 minutes. Add the bread flour, ½ cup at a time, beating on low speed until a soft dough that clears the sides of the bowl forms, switching to a wooden spoon when necessary if making by hand.

3. Turn the dough out onto a lightly floured work surface and knead to form a soft, springy dough that is resilient to the touch, 1 to 2 minutes for a machine-mixed dough and 3 to 4 minutes for a hand-mixed dough, dusting with flour only 1 tablespoon at a time, just enough as needed to prevent sticking. Place in a lightly greased deep container, turn once to coat the top, and cover with plastic wrap. Let rise at room temperature until double in bulk, 1½ to 2 hours.

continued

4. Meanwhile, preheat an oven to 350°F. Spread the hazelnuts in a single layer on a baking sheet and bake until lightly colored and the skins blister, 10 to 12 minutes. Let cool. Wrap the nuts in a clean kitchen towel and rub to remove the skins. Chop coarsely and set aside.

5. Grease two 8½-by-4½-inch loaf pans. Turn the dough out onto the work surface, pat into a large oval, and sprinkle evenly with the toasted hazelnuts. Roll the dough and knead into a ball to distribute the hazelnuts. Divide into 2 equal portions. Pat each portion into a rectangle and roll into a loaf shape. Place in the pans, seam side down, and cover loosely with plastic wrap. Let rise until double in bulk, about 1 hour.

6. About 20 minutes before baking, preheat an oven to 375°F and position a rack in the center of the oven.

7. Using a sharp knife, make 3 diagonal slashes no more than ¼ inch deep down the center of each loaf. Bake for 45 to 50 minutes, or until the tops are brown and crusty and the loaves sound hollow when tapped with a finger. Remove from the pans to cool on a rack.

Bread-Machine Chestnut Bread with Hazelnuts

1½-pound loaf

½ cup whole hazelnuts

1 cup plus 2 tablespoons water

2 tablespoons honey

3 tablespoons olive oil

¼ cup nonfat dry milk powder

2 cups bread flour

⅔ cup white whole-wheat flour

⅓ cup chestnut flour

4 teaspoons vital wheat gluten

1 teaspoon salt

2 teaspoons bread machine yeast

1-pound loaf

⅓ cup whole hazelnuts

⅞ cup water

1 tablespoon honey

2 tablespoons olive oil

3 tablespoons nonfat dry milk powder

1¼ cups bread flour

½ cup white whole-wheat flour

¼ cup chestnut flour

3 teaspoons vital wheat gluten

½ teaspoon salt

1½ teaspoons bread machine yeast

1. Preheat an oven to 350°F. Spread the hazelnuts in a single layer on a baking sheet and bake until lightly colored and the skins blister, 10 to 12 minutes. Let cool. Wrap the nuts in a clean kitchen towel and rub to remove the skins. Chop coarsely and set aside.

2. Place all the ingredients, except the nuts, in the pan according to the manufacturer's instructions. Set crust on medium and program for the fruit and nut cycle or the basic bread cycle; press Start. At the beep, add the nuts at midcycle. Or, if using the basic bread cycle, mix all the ingredients together.

3. After the baking cycle ends, remove the bread from the pan and place on a rack to cool.

This coarse-textured, mild-flavored bread is best served warm from the toaster with honey butter. The dough is really a stiff batter and does not require kneading. Slices of the toasted bread are also good as the base for eggs Benedict.

Chestnut Toasting Bread

Makes two 7-by-3½-inch loaves

1 tablespoon (1 package) active dry yeast

½ cup nonfat dry milk powder

2½ teaspoons salt

1 cup chestnut flour

3¼ to 3½ cups bread flour

2 cups hot water (120°F)

2 tablespoons honey

2 tablespoons unsalted butter, melted

1 large egg

⅓ cup white cornmeal or coarse semolina, for sprinkling

½ teaspoon baking soda dissolved in 1 tablespoon warm water

Honey Butter (recipe follows)

1. In a large bowl using a whisk or in the bowl of a heavy-duty electric mixer fitted with the paddle attachment, combine the yeast, milk powder, salt, chestnut flour, and 1 cup of the bread flour. Add the hot water and beat hard to combine. Add the honey, butter, egg, and remaining bread flour, ½ cup at a time, until a moist, smooth dough that pulls away from the sides of the bowl in thick liquid ribbons forms, switching to a wooden spoon if making by hand. Cover the bowl with plastic wrap and let rise at warm room temperature until double in bulk and bubbly, 1 to 1½ hours.

2. Generously butter two 7-by-3½-inch loaf pans and sprinkle with cornmeal. Gently stir down the dough. Add the dissolved baking soda and stir well to incorporate. Divide among the prepared pans, filling each three-fourths full. Sprinkle the tops with cornmeal. Cover lightly with plastic wrap and let rise until the dough is level with the rims of the pans, about 1 hour.

3. About 20 minutes before baking, preheat an oven to 375°F and position a rack in the center of the oven.

4. Bake for 30 to 35 minutes, or until the tops are golden brown and the sides slightly contract from the

continued

pans. Let stand for 5 minutes before removing from the pans to cool on a rack. Cut into ¾-inch slices, and serve with Honey Butter.

Honey Butter

Makes about ¾ cup

> ½ cup (1 stick) unsalted butter, at room temperature, cut into pieces
>
> ⅓ cup honey
>
> Dash of ground cinnamon
>
> Dash of nutmeg

In a small bowl, cream the butter, honey, and spices, using a wooden spoon or handheld electric mixer, until smooth. Transfer to a small container, cover, and refrigerate until serving. Store in the refrigerator for up to 2 months.

Chickpea

Chickpeas, also known as garbanzos or cecis, have been cultivated for so long in the Mediterranean, India, and Egypt that no wild species has ever been found. It is known, however, through archaeological diggings, that a wild species existed in the seventh millennium B.C. in the Languedoc region of southern France. Chickpeas were a preferred cultivated vegetable in the Tigris and Euphrates Valleys. Cultivated chickpeas were brought by Phoenician sailors from western Asia to the Iberian Peninsula and became a desired vegetable as far away as South America.

Many fragrant chickpea breads are regional preferences. Fritters are popular in France and the Middle East. In the south of France, a chickpea flour pancake is a delicious seaside snack with wine. On the Italian Riviera, a cross between a bread and a pasta is baked in a hot oven and served with plenty of freshly ground black pepper and sliced artichokes or raw onions. Thick toasted wedges of chickpea bread are eaten with cheese and jam for breakfast in Greece. In India and Pakistan, flour ground from chickpeas or lentils is used with some whole-wheat flour to make griddle flatbreads similar to tortillas.

Chickpea flour is ground from beans that are first lightly heated and gently toasted under radiant heat. It is not an easy flour to find; look in natural-food and Indian grocery stores, or order by mail.

Fromage blanc, *a French-style spreadable skim-milk cheese, is similar to cream cheese and kefir cheese, but without fat. Its tangy taste and soft texture, along with the sweetness of orange marmalade, offer a surprise when you bite into a warm muffin.*

Chickpea Muffins with Marmalade and Fromage Blanc

Makes 10 muffins

1½ cups chickpea flour

1 cup unbleached all-purpose flour

¼ cup sugar

Grated zest and juice of 1 orange

2½ teaspoons baking powder

½ teaspoon salt

1 cup milk

3 large eggs

6 tablespoons (¾ stick) unsalted butter, melted, or ⅓ cup canola oil

¼ cup fromage blanc

¼ cup orange marmalade

1. Preheat an oven to 375°F and position a rack in the center of the oven. Grease 10 standard muffin cups.

2. In a large bowl, combine the chickpea and all-purpose flours, sugar, zest, baking powder, and salt. In another bowl, combine the milk, orange juice, eggs, and butter with a whisk or an electric mixer until blended. Add to the dry ingredients, stirring with a large spatula just until moistened, using no more than 15 to 20 strokes.

3. Spoon the batter into each prepared muffin cup until half full. Place 1 rounded teaspoon of the fromage blanc in the center and top with 1 teaspoon of the marmalade. Add batter to fill level with the top of the cups.

4. Bake for 18 to 22 minutes, or until the tops are browned and feel dry and springy, and a cake tester inserted into the center comes out clean. Let the muffins rest in the pan for 5 minutes before removing to a rack. Serve warm.

On the French Riviera, street vendors sell socca, *the Niçoise flatbread pancake made from chickpea flour in rounds almost 2 feet in diameter. For a home version, the pancakes are smaller and baked in an oven. Serve in wedges, drizzled with a very fruity extra-virgin olive oil and sprinkled with a few twists of freshly ground black pepper, as a unique hors d'oeuvre.*

Niçoise Chickpea Pancakes

Makes 3 pancakes

1¾ cups chickpea flour

½ teaspoon ground cumin

½ teaspoon sea salt

1½ cups water

¼ cup extra-virgin olive oil, plus oil for serving

Black pepper, for serving

1. In a bowl using a whisk or immersion blender or in the bowl of a heavy-duty electric mixer fitted with the whisk attachment, combine the flour, cumin, salt, water, and ¼ cup oil. Beat hard for 1 minute. Cover and let stand at room temperature for 1 hour.

2. Preheat an oven to 425°F and position a rack in the top third of the oven. Generously brush three 9-inch round cake pans with olive oil.

3. Divide the batter among the pans, tilting to coat the entire bottom. Bake for 25 to 30 minutes, or until golden and crisp. Place the pans on a rack. Using a wide spatula, remove the pancakes to a work surface. Using a sharp knife, cut into 4 wedges. Drizzle with olive oil, sprinkle with a few grinds of freshly ground pepper, and serve immediately.

important addition to gluten-free breads when combined with other flours such as rice flour, tapioca starch (or cassava flour, long a staple tuber crop in equatorial America and Florida), or arrowroot (another easily digestible starchy tuber flour, originally from Brazil). These tasty gluten-free flour mixtures can be substituted cup for cup in wheat flour recipes with great success. Potato flour, which is quite dense, cannot be substituted for potato starch. Mealy-textured, high-starch potato varieties, marketed as Idaho or russets, are the best for the mashed potatoes called for in breads.

Potato

The potato is a member of the nightshade family, which also includes tomatoes, eggplants, and peppers. It is a portion of the underground stem of the plant, hence the French name *pomme de terre*, or "apple of the earth." *Tuber*, derived from the Latin for "swelling," is an apt descriptive label that has stuck to this day. About 1,000 varieties of potatoes in almost a rainbow of colors are grown today.

Yeast loves the enzymes and starch in potatoes, so many sourdough starters and yeast doughs contain potato. Breads made with potatoes remain fresh a few days longer than other loaves. Potatoes and potato flour make a substandard bread on their own, but when combined with wheat flour result in a wonderful moist bread. Potato flour, a staple in old-fashioned kitchens, is known for giving sweetness and body to breads, since the starch it contains is the same as found in true grains.

Potato flour is finely ground from dehydrated starchy potatoes. It is not interchangeable with instant mashed potato flakes. The starch, also packaged as potato starch flour, is a very fine white flour that is excellent for baking breads, muffins, pie crusts, and cakes when combined with other specialty flours and gluten flour. Use the starch like cornstarch for making a glossy glaze for whole-grain bread or for dusting loaf breads just before baking. Potato starch flour is an

Potatoes combined with eggs results in particularly moist, fluffy loaves that are less sweet than regular challah. Slices of the bread make fabulous French toast and grilled sandwiches the day after baking. This is a family-sized recipe, so plan accordingly. It can easily be halved.

Potato Challah

Makes 2 large free-form loaves or four 9-by-5-inch loaves

2 to 3 large (about 1½ pounds) Russet potatoes, peeled and cut into large pieces

2 cups water

1½ tablespoons (scant 2 packages) active dry yeast

10 to 11 cups unbleached all-purpose or bread flour

4 teaspoons salt

2 tablespoons honey

4 tablespoons (½ stick) unsalted butter, melted

4 extra-large eggs

1 egg beaten with 1 teaspoon water, for glaze

2 tablespoons sesame seeds or poppyseeds, for sprinkling

1. Place the potatoes and water in a 2-quart saucepan. Bring to a boil, reduce the heat to simmer, cover, and cook until tender, about 20 minutes. Drain and reserve the liquid, adding more water if necessary to make 1¼ cups. Mash the potatoes, then set aside to cool. Warm or cool the potato water to 105° to 115°F and pour ½ cup into a small bowl. Sprinkle the yeast over the potato water. Stir to dissolve and let stand until foamy, about 10 minutes.

2. In a large bowl using a whisk or in the bowl of a heavy-duty electric mixer fitted with a paddle attachment, combine 2 cups of the all-purpose flour and the salt, honey, butter, mashed potatoes, and yeast-potato water. Beat hard until creamy, 1 minute. Add the eggs and beat for 2 minutes. Add the remaining all-purpose flour, ½ cup at a time, beating on low speed until a soft, shaggy dough that just clears the sides of the bowl forms, switching to a wooden spoon when necessary if making by hand.

3. Turn the dough out onto a lightly floured work surface and knead until soft and springy, 1 to 3 minutes for a machine-mixed dough and 3 to 5 minutes for a hand-mixed dough, dusting with flour only 1 tablespoon at a

continued

time, just enough as needed to prevent sticking. Place in a lightly greased deep container, turn once to coat the top, and cover with plastic wrap. Let rise at room temperature until double in bulk, 1 to 1½ hours. Do not allow to rise more, as the dough has a tendency to tear.

4. Grease 2 baking sheets or line with parchment paper. Turn the dough out onto a lightly floured work surface and divide into 6 equal portions. With the palms of your hands, roll into 6 ropes about 14 inches long, tapering them at each end. Gently dust with flour. Place 3 of the ropes side by side and braid. Tuck the ends under and pinch into tapered points. Repeat to form second loaf. Alternatively, divide the dough into 4 equal portions, shape into rectangular loaves, and place in 4 greased or parchment-lined loaf pans. Cover loosely with plastic wrap and let rise until almost double in bulk, about 45 minutes.

5. About 20 minutes before baking, preheat an oven to 400°F and position a rack in the center of the oven.

6. Brush the loaves with the egg glaze and sprinkle with the seeds. Place in the oven and reduce the temperature to 350°F. Bake for 40 to 45 minutes, or until the loaves are deep golden brown and sound hollow when tapped with your finger. Remove from the sheets to a rack to cool.

Bread-Machine Potato Challah

1½-pound loaf

1 medium (about 9 ounces) Russet potato, cut into chunks

2 tablespoons unsalted butter, melted

1½ tablespoons honey

1 large egg

3 cups bread flour

1½ teaspoons vital wheat gluten

1 teaspoon salt

1¾ teaspoons bread machine yeast

1-pound loaf

1 medium (about 7 ounces) Russet potato, cut into chunks

1½ tablespoons unsalted butter, melted

1 tablespoon honey

1 large egg

2 cups bread flour

1 teaspoon vital wheat gluten

¾ teaspoon salt

1½ teaspoons bread machine yeast

1. Place the potatoes in a saucepan and add water to cover. Bring to a boil, reduce the heat to simmer, cover, and cook until tender, about 10 minutes. Drain and reserve the liquid, adding more water if necessary to make ½ cup if preparing a 1½-pound loaf or ⅓ cup if preparing a 1-pound loaf. Peel and mash the potato, then set aside to cool to room temperature. You will have about ¾ cup mashed potato for the 1½-pound loaf and ½ cup for the 1-pound loaf.

2. Place the potato water, mashed potato, and remaining ingredients in the pan according to the manufacturer's instructions. Set crust on medium and program for the basic or tender bread cycle; press Start.

3. After the baking cycle ends, remove the bread from the pan and place on a rack to cool.

This beautifully domed, earthy loaf has a soft, fluffy crumb. Be certain to purée the potatoes well, as any lumps will be evident with the first bite. For a variation (recipe follows), the dough incorporates prosciutto and is baked into a flat loaf that is best served hot, pulled apart with your fingers. If you own a baking stone, use it for baking these loaves.

Potato Country Bread

Makes 1 large round loaf

1 large (8 to 10 ounces) russet potato, peeled and cut into large pieces

2 cups water

1 tablespoon (1 package) active dry yeast

Pinch of sugar

1 tablespoon vital wheat gluten, optional

½ cup potato flour

3 to 3½ cups bread flour

2 tablespoons olive oil

2 teaspoons salt

1. Place the potato and water in a 2-quart saucepan. Bring to a boil, reduce the heat to simmer, cover, and cook until soft, about 20 minutes. Drain and reserve the liquid, adding more water as necessary to make 1¼ cups. Mash the potato and set aside to cool. Warm or cool the potato water to 105° to 115°F and pour into a small bowl. Sprinkle the yeast and sugar over the potato water. Stir to dissolve and let stand until foamy, about 10 minutes.

2. In a large bowl using a whisk or in the bowl of a heavy-duty electric mixer fitted with a paddle attachment, combine the gluten (if using), potato flour, 1 cup of the bread flour, oil, salt, mashed potatoes, and yeast-potato water. Beat hard until creamy, 2 minutes. Add the remaining bread flour, ½ cup at a time, beating on low speed until a soft, shaggy dough that just clears the sides of the bowl forms, switching to a wooden spoon when necessary if making by hand.

3. Turn the dough out onto a lightly floured work surface and knead until soft and springy, 1 to 3 minutes for a machine-mixed dough and 3 to 5 minutes for a hand-mixed dough, dusting with flour only 1 tablespoon at a time, just enough as needed to prevent sticking. Do not add too much flour or the loaf will be very heavy. Place in a lightly greased deep container,

turn once to coat the top, and cover with plastic wrap. Let rise at room temperature until double in bulk, 1 to 1½ hours.

4. Line a baking sheet with parchment paper and dust with potato flour. Turn the dough out onto a lightly floured work surface and knead into a tight round. Dust with potato flour and place on the baking sheet. Cover loosely with plastic wrap and let rise until puffy, about 30 minutes.

5. About 20 minutes before baking, preheat an oven to 425°F and position a rack in the center of the oven.

6. Using a sharp knife, make 3 diagonal slashes no more than ¼ inch deep across the top of the loaf. Bake for 15 minutes, reduce the oven temperature to 375°F, and bake for 30 to 35 minutes longer, or until the loaves are deep golden brown and sound hollow when tapped with your finger. Remove from the sheet to a rack to cool.

Potato *Prosciutto Fougasse:*

While mixing the dough in step 2, add 2 ounces thinly sliced and chopped prosciutto. Knead and rise as directed. Line a large baking sheet with parchment paper and dust with potato flour. Turn the dough out onto a floured work surface and, using a rolling pin, roll into a rectangle about 10 by 14 inches. Transfer to the prepared sheet. Using a sharp knife, make 4 to 6 diagonal cuts down the center, cutting through to the pan. Pull the dough slightly to open and exaggerate the cuts. Brush the dough with some olive oil. Cover loosely with plastic wrap and let rise until double in bulk, about 20 minutes. Bake in a preheated 425°F oven for 20 to 25 minutes, or until golden brown and dry to the touch. Makes 1 rectangular flat loaf.

Soybean

The Chinese call soybeans the "treasure-house of life," recognition of their perfect balance of carbohydrates, all the amino acids, polyunsaturated fats, mineral salts, a sugar similar to lactose, and vitamins. The origins of the soybean plant are lost in antiquity, but the first references occur in the sixth century B.C. in a book of Chinese royal court poems. To this day, soybeans are a staple on the Asian continent. More soybeans are now grown in the United States than anywhere else.

Soybeans were long thought unsuitable for bread making. On their own, they make moist, compact bricks with a hearty, musty, sweet flavor. Soy flour, however, complements other flours, slows rancidity in baked goods, and adds considerable nutrition and moisture to loaves. Breads with soy flour are chewy with a golden crust and a delicate flavor. The flour also makes great pancakes, biscuits, and muffins.

Soy products for baking include grits (coarse-ground pieces used for cereal), soy flakes (steamed and rolled dry-roasted whole soybeans), and soy meal (rough-ground flour). My favorite is a stone-milled flour finely ground from toasted whole soybeans. The best-tasting, most nutritious flour is stone-ground and full-fat. The defatted flour, a by-product of soy oil extraction, is highly refined; the oil is removed by a process using chemical solvents, and the resulting flour is less satisfactory in baking.

Known originally as Cornell Triple-Rich Fifty-Fifty Bread, this revolutionary bread boasts three nutritious ingredients: soy flour, wheat germ, and nonfat dry milk. It really has five, including the egg and nutritional yeast. My version has extra gluten for enhanced texture and uses a sponge to help make a superior-flavored loaf.

Cornell Wonder Bread

Makes two 9-by-5-inch loaves

Sponge

3 cups warm water (105° to 115°F)

¾ cup nonfat dry milk powder

2 tablespoons (2 packages) active dry yeast

¼ cup packed light brown sugar

¼ cup honey

3 cups whole-wheat flour

Dough

3 tablespoons canola oil

1 large egg

4 teaspoons salt

2 tablespoons nutritional yeast

2 tablespoons vital wheat gluten

3 tablespoons wheat germ

¾ cup full-fat stone-ground soy flour

2½ to 3½ cups bread flour

1. **To make the sponge:** In a large bowl using a whisk or in the bowl of a heavy-duty electric mixer fitted with the whisk attachment, combine the water, milk powder, yeast, sugar, honey, and whole-wheat flour and beat until smooth. Scrape down the sides with a spatula and cover with plastic wrap. Set in a warm place until double in bulk and bubbly, about 1 hour. Gently stir down with a wooden spoon.

2. **To make the dough:** Add the oil, egg, salt, nutritional yeast, gluten, wheat germ, soy flour, and 1 cup of the bread flour to the sponge and beat hard by hand with a wooden spoon for 2 minutes (at least 100 strokes) or with a mixer on medium speed until smooth. Add the remaining bread flour, ½ cup at a time, beating on low speed until a very soft, thick batterlike dough that just clears the sides of the bowl forms, about 5 minutes.

3. Turn the dough out onto a lightly floured work surface and knead until soft, springy and slightly moist, 2 to 3 minutes for a machine-mixed dough and 3 to 5 minutes for a hand-mixed dough, dusting with flour only 1 tablespoon at a time, just enough as needed to prevent sticking. Place in a lightly greased deep container, turn once to coat the top, and cover with plastic

continued

wrap. Let rise at room temperature until double in bulk, 1½ to 2 hours. Gently deflate and let rise, covered, for 30 minutes longer.

4. Generously grease two 9-by-5-inch loaf pans. Turn the dough onto the work surface and divide into 2 equal portions. Pat each into a rectangle and roll into a loaf shape. Place, seam side down, in the prepared pans. Cover loosely with plastic wrap and let rise until not quite double in bulk and even with the rims of the pans, 45 minutes to 1 hour.

5. About 20 minutes before baking, preheat an oven to 350°F and position a rack in the center of the oven.

6. Bake for 50 to 55 minutes, or until the tops are deep brown and the loaves sound hollow when tapped with your finger. Place aluminum foil over the tops to control excess browning, if necessary. Remove from the pans to a rack to cool.

Bread-Machine Cornell Wonder Bread

1½-pound loaf

1¼ cups water

2 tablespoons oil

2 tablespoons honey

2 tablespoons packed light brown sugar

1 large egg

1½ cups whole-wheat flour

1 cup plus 2 tablespoons bread flour

⅓ cup soy flour

1½ tablespoons wheat germ

¼ cup nonfat dry milk powder

5 teaspoons vital wheat gluten

1 teaspoon salt

2¼ teaspoons bread machine yeast

1-pound loaf

⅞ cup water

1½ tablespoons oil

1½ tablespoons honey

1½ tablespoons packed light brown sugar

1 large egg

1 cup whole-wheat flour

¾ cup bread flour

¼ cup soy flour

1 tablespoon wheat germ

3 tablespoons nonfat dry milk powder

3 teaspoons vital wheat gluten

¾ teaspoon salt

1½ teaspoons bread machine yeast

1. Place all of the ingredients in the pan according to the manufacturer's instructions. Set crust on medium and program for the whole-wheat bread cycle; press Start. If using the basic bread cycle, after the first rise cycle, reset, allowing the dough to rise a second time.

2. After the baking cycle ends, remove the bread from the pan and place on a rack to cool.

Biscuits are as special as they are simple. If you love biscuits, these old-fashioned dinner gems will give the bright flavor, flaky texture, and soul-satisfying feeling only home baking can provide.

Green and Golden Biscuits

Makes 12 biscuits

1 cup unbleached all-purpose flour

⅔ cup whole-wheat pastry flour

⅓ cup full-fat stone-ground soy flour

2 tablespoons coarsely chopped watercress

2 tablespoons coarsely chopped Italian parsley

1 tablespoon baking powder

½ teaspoon salt

5 tablespoons unsalted butter or soy margarine, cut into pieces

2 large eggs

About ⅓ cup half-and-half or plain soy milk

1 to 2 tablespoons sesame seeds

1. In a bowl, combine the all-purpose, whole-wheat, and soy flours, watercress, parsley, baking powder, and salt. Cut in the butter with a pastry blender or 2 knives until coarse crumbs are formed. Stir in the eggs and half-and-half, mixing until a soft dough forms.

2. Preheat an oven to 400°F and position a rack in the center of the oven. Grease a baking sheet or line with parchment paper.

3. Turn the dough out onto a lightly floured work surface and knead gently until the dough just holds together, about 10 times. Roll or pat the dough into a rectangle about ¾ inch thick. Do not add too much flour or the biscuits will be tough. Sprinkle with the sesame seeds and press into the dough. Using a sharp knife or pastry wheel, form 12 squares. Alternatively, using a 2½-inch biscuit cutter, press firmly without twisting to make biscuits. Cut out biscuits as close together as possible for a minimum of leftover dough. Press the scraps gently together and cut out additional biscuits. Place, ½ inch apart, on the prepared sheet.

4. Bake for 12 to 15 minutes, or until golden brown. Let rest on the sheet for a few minutes and serve hot.

Bread-Machine Cracked-Soy Sandwich Bread

1½-pound loaf

⅓ cup soy grits

1¼ cups boiling water

2 tablespoons honey

3 tablespoons unsalted butter

1¾ cups bread flour

½ cup whole-wheat flour

½ cup soy flour

⅓ cup dry buttermilk powder

1½ tablespoons vital wheat gluten

1 teaspoon salt

2¼ teaspoons bread machine yeast

1-pound loaf

¼ cup soy grits

1 cup boiling water

1½ tablespoons honey

2 tablespoons unsalted butter

1 cup bread flour

⅓ cup whole-wheat flour

⅓ cup soy flour

¼ cup dry buttermilk powder

1 tablespoon vital wheat gluten

¾ teaspoon salt

2 teaspoons bread machine yeast

1. Place the grits in a bowl and add the boiling water. Add the honey and butter. Let stand for 1 hour to soften.

2. Place the remaining ingredients and the soaked grits and their liquid in the pan according to the manufacturer's instructions. Set crust on medium and program for the whole-wheat bread cycle; press Start. If using the basic bread cycle, after the first rise cycle, reset, allowing the dough to rise a second time.

3. After the baking cycle ends, remove the bread from the pan and place on a rack to cool.

Mail-Order Granary

The following sources can provide the home baker with a wide variety of whole grains and flours, many of which can be difficult to find even in the best-stocked stores.

Arrowhead Mills, for decades a main source of mail-order grains, has discontinued this service because the company's flours are so widely available in stores. Mountain Ark Trading Company specializes in macrobiotic grains. Goldmine Natural Foods and Bob's Red Mill are becoming bigger names in the mail-order grain business, and King Arthur, Pamela's Products, and Walnut Acres offer one-stop shopping. Call or write these and the other businesses for complete catalog and price list.

Bob's Red Mill
Natural Foods, Inc.
5209 S.E. International Way
Milwaukee, OR 97222
503-645-3215

Butte Creek Mill
P.O. Box 561
Eagle Point, OR 97524
503-826-3531

Goldmine Natural Foods Company
3419 Hancock Street
San Diego, CA 92110-4307
1-800-475-FOOD

King Arthur Flour
P.O. Box 876
Norwich, VT 05055
1-800-827-6836

Mountain Ark Trading Company
799 Old Leicester Highway
Asheville, NC 28806
1-800-643-8909

Pamela's Products Inc. (Guisto's Mail-Order Source for the Home Baker)
156 Utah Avenue
South San Francisco, CA 94080
415-952-4546

Walnut Acres
Walnut Acres Road
Penns Creek, PA 17862
800-344-9025

Amaranth
Larry Walters and his brother have been processing and marketing most of the amaranth in the United States since 1983.

Nu-World Amaranth, Inc.
P.O. Box 2202
Naperville, IL 60567
630-369-6819

Barley
Western Trails offers the most innovative barley available today. The Black Buffalo and Bronze Nugget barleys, either whole or as flour, are a must.

Western Trails Food Products
P.O. Box 460
Bozeman, MT 59715
406-587-5489

Buckwheat

Birkett Mills is the major processor of buckwheat products in the United States today. The company's flour and kasha are marketed under the trade name "Pocono." A pale, mild-flavored Silverskin buckwheat Ployes de Boquite *pancake mix, a centuries-old Acadian bread substitute, is available from the Bouchard Family Farm.*

Birkett Mills/The National Buckwheat Institute
P.O. Box 440
Penn Yan, NY 14527
315-536-3391

Bouchard Family Farm
R.F.D. #1, Box 690
Fort Kent, ME 04743
207-834-3237

Corn

Blue cornmeals, blue corn masa harina, and the most flavorful stone-ground masa harina are best mail-ordered from New Mexico. I buy both masas from Santa Fe School of Cooking. I especially like the cornmeals from Butte Creek Mill in Oregon and Kenyon and Gray's mills in Rhode Island, which are ground from Narragansett Indian flint corn, the corn grown by the first New England colonists.

Gray's Grist Mill
Box 422
Adamsville, RI 02801
508-636-6075

Kenyon Cornmeal Company
P.O. Box 221
West Kingston, RI 02892
401-783-4054

Los Chileros de Neuvo Mexico
P.O. Box 6215
Santa Fe, NM 87502
505-471-6967

Santa Fe School of Cooking
116 W. San Francisco Street
Santa Fe, NM 87501
505-983-4511

Kamut

Montana Flour and Grain is the only company in the United States that grows kamut. All available flour is organic.

Kamut Association of America
Montana Flour and Grain
P.O. Box 691
Ft. Benton, MT 59442
800-644-6450

Oats

Although commercial oatmeals and Irish oatmeals are very easy to find in every supermarket, organic brands will amaze you with their texture and nutty flavor. Grain Millers is a great family-run company that specializes in distributing organic oats.

Grain Millers
11100 NE Eighth, Suite 710
Bellevue, WA 98009
800-443-8972

Quinoa and Potatoes

White quinoa and black quinoa from Ernie New in the San Luis Valley are available from White Mountain Farm. In the fall, the farm offers organic potato gift boxes.

White Mountain Farm
8890 Lane 4 North
Mosca, CO 81146
800-364-3019

Rice

This is the only great source for specialty rices and rice blends, selling wehani, American basmati, japonica black rice, brown rices, and arborio varieties.

Lundberg Family Farms
P.O. Box 369
Richvale, CA 95974
916-882-4551

Teff

Wayne Carlson's Teff Company is the only commercial company growing and marketing this grain, under the moniker of Maskal Teff. He supplies the natural-foods stores through Bob's Red Mill and Ancient Harvest. He also grinds and packages teff flour for the Ethiopian community.

The Teff Company
P. O. Box A
Caldwell, ID 83606
208-455-0375

Wild Rice

When Cook's Illustrated Magazine *did taste tests of the best cultivated brands of wild rice, the favorites included Gibbs and St. Maries (the mildest flavored). Gibbs in Minnesota carries hard-to-find wild rice flour.*

Gibbs Wild Rice
10400 Billings Road
Live Oak, CA 95053
800-824-4932

Gibbs Wild Rice
Route 2
Dear River, MN 56636
800-344-6378

Manitok Organic Wild Rice Cooperative
Box 97
Callaway, MN 56521
800-726-1863

St. Maries Wild Rice
P.O. Box 293
St. Maries, ID 83861
800-225-9453

Index